Books by Robert Penn Warren

JOHN BROWN: THE MAKING OF A MARTYR

THIRTY-SIX POEMS

NIGHT RIDER

ELEVEN POEMS ON THE SAME THEME

AT HEAVEN'S GATE

SELECTED POEMS, 1923–1943

ALL THE KING'S MEN

BLACKBERRY WINTER

THE CIRCUS IN THE ATTIC

WORLD ENOUGH AND TIME

BROTHER TO DRAGONS

BAND OF ANGELS

SEGREGATION: THE INNER CONFLICT IN THE SOUTH

PROMISES: POEMS 1954–1956

SELECTED ESSAYS

THE CAVE

ALL THE KING'S MEN (play)

YOU, EMPERORS, AND OTHERS: POEMS 1957–1960

THE LEGACY OF THE CIVIL WAR

WILDERNESS

FLOOD

WHO SPEAKS FOR THE NEGRO?

SELECTED POEMS: NEW AND OLD 1923–1966

SELECTED POEMS
New and Old 1923–1966

Selected Poems:

NEW AND OLD, 1923-1966

ROBERT PENN WARREN

RANDOM HOUSE   NEW YORK

ACKNOWLEDGMENT

The poems in this volume that have not previously been published in book form appeared first in the following periodicals (the page numbers in parentheses refer to pages in this book and indicate which poems appeared in each):

Encounter (*pp. 19–39, 58–66*), The New Leader (*pp. 67–68*), The New Yorker (*pp. 3, 6–7, 9–12, 40–49, 52–57*), The New York Review of Books (*pp. 8, 50–51, 81, 84–85, 90–91*), Partisan Review (*p. 5*), The Sewanee Review (*pp. 13–18*), The Saturday Review (*pp. 82–83, 86–89*), The Yale Review (*pp. 69–80*).

To **ELEANOR, ROSANNA,** *and* **GABRIEL**

PREFATORY NOTE

I have published five volumes of poems, not including a long poem presented independently. Here I have gathered, in addition to a considerable number of new pieces, those from the five earlier volumes which seem to lie on the main line of my impulse. Many of the poems in this volume have been revised, some of them drastically. But in revising old poems, I have tried not to tamper with meanings, only to sharpen old meanings—for poems are, in one perspective at least, always a life record, and live their own life by that fact.

Stratton, Vermont,
March 6, 1966

Contents

ix

xi

From SELECTED POEMS
1923–1943

TALE OF TIME
New Poems   1960–1966

※ This symbol is used to indicate a space between sections of a poem wherever such spaces are lost in pagination.

NOTES ON A LIFE TO BE LIVED

I Stargazing

The stars are only a backdrop for
The human condition, the stars
Are brilliant above the black spruces,
And fall comes on. Wind

Does not move in the star-stillness, wind
Is afraid of itself, as you have been afraid in
Those moments when destruction and revelation
Have spat at each other like cats, and the mirror
Showed no breath, ha, ha, and the wind,

Far off in arctic starlight, is afraid
To breathe, and waits, huddled in
Sparse blackness of spruces, black glitter in starlight, in
A land, north, where snow already is, and waits:

And the girl is saying, "You do not look
At the stars," for I did not look at
The stars, for I know they are there, know
That if I look at the stars, I

Will have to live over again all I have lived
In the years I looked at stars and
Cried out, "O reality!" The stars
Love me. I love them. I wish they

Loved God, too. I truly wish that.

3

I I Small White House

The sun of July beats down on the small white house.
The pasture is brown-bright as brass, and like brass, sings with heat.
Halt! And I stand here, hills shudder, withdraw into distance,
Like paranoia. And a child's cry comes from the house.

Tell me, oh, where, in what state, did I see the small white house,
Which I see in my mind?—And the wax-wing's beak slices the blue cedar-berry,
Which is as blue as distance. The river, far off, shrinks
Among the hot boulders, no glister, looks dead as a discarded snake-skin
                                        rubbed off on stone. The house

Swims in that dazzle of no-Time. The child's cry comes from the house.

4

I I I   Blow, West Wind

I know, I know—though the evidence
Is lost, and the last who might speak are dead.
Blow, west wind, blow, and the evidence, O,

Is lost, and wind shakes the cedar, and O,
I know how the kestrel hung over Wyoming,
Breast reddened in sunset, and O, the cedar

Shakes, and I know how cold
Was the sweat on my father's mouth, dead.
Blow, west wind, blow, shake the cedar, I know

How once I, a boy, crouching at creekside,
Watched, in the sunlight, a handful of water
Drip, drip, from my hand. The drops—they were bright!

But you believe nothing, with the evidence lost.

5

I V Composition in Gold and Red-Gold

Between the event and the word, golden
The sunlight falls, between
The brown brook's braiding and the mountain it
Falls, in pitiless plenitude, and every leaf
On the ruined apple tree is gold, and the apples all
Gold, too, especially those

On the ground. The gold of apples
That have fallen flushes to flame, but
Gold is the flame. Gold
Goes red-gold—and the scene:

A chipmunk is under the apple tree, sits up
Among gold apples, is
Golden in gold light. The chipmunk
Wriggles its small black nose
In the still center of the world of light.

The hair of the little girl is as brown-gold as
Brook water braiding in sunlight.

The cat, crouching by the gray stone, is gold, too.
The tail of the cat, half-Persian, weaves from side to side,
In infinite luxury, gold plume
Of sea-weed in that tide of light.
That is a motion that puts
The world to sleep.

The eyes of the cat are gold, and

※

I want to sleep. But
The event: the tiny
Shriek unstitches the afternoon, the girl
Screams, the sky
Tingles crystalline like a struck wine glass, and you
Feel the salt thickening, like grit, in your secret blood. Afterward

There is a difference in the quality of silence.
Every leaf, gold, hangs motionless on the tree, but
There is a difference in the quality of
Motionlessness: unverbed, unverved, they
Hang. On the last day will the sun
Explode? Or simply get too tired?

The chipmunk lies gold among the apples.
It is prone and totally relaxed like ripe
Fruit fallen, and,
Upon closer inspection, you can see
The faint smear of flame-gold at the base
Of the skull. This effect
Completes the composition.

The little girl
Holds the cat in her arms,
Crooning, "Baby, oh, baby." She weeps under
The powerful flood of gold light.

Somewhere, in the shade of alders, a trout
Hangs steady, head against a current like ice.

The eagle I had earlier seen climbing
The light above the mountain is

Now beyond sight.

V Little Boy and Lost Shoe

The little boy lost his shoe in the field.
Home he hobbled, not caring, with a stick whipping goldenrod.
Go find that shoe—I mean it, right now!
And he went, not now singing, and the field was big.

Under the sky he walked and the sky was big.
Sunlight touched the goldenrod, and yellowed his hair,
But the sun was low now, and oh, he should know
He must hurry to find that shoe, or the sun will be down.

Oh, hurry, boy, for the grass will be tall as a tree.
Hurry, for the moon has bled, but not like a heart, in pity.
Hurry, for time is money and the sun is low.
Yes, damn it, hurry, for shoes cost money, you know.

I don't know why you dawdle and do not hurry.
The mountains are leaning their heads together to watch.
How dilatory can a boy be, I ask you? Off in Wyoming,
The mountains lean. They watch. They know.

V I   Patriotic Tour and Postulate of Joy

Once, once, in Washington,
D.C., in June,
All night—I swear it—a single mockingbird
Sang,
Sang to the Presidential ear,
Wherein it poured
Such criticism and advice as that ear
Had rarely had the privilege to hear.

And sang to every senator
Available,
And some, as sources best informed affirm,
Rose,
Rose with a taste in the throat like bile,
To the bathroom fled
And spat, and faced the mirror there, and while
The bicarb fizzed, stared, feet cold on tile.

And sang to Edgar Hoover, too,
And as it preached
Subversion and all bright disaster, he
Woke;
Woke, then looked at Mom's photo, so heard
No more. But far,
Far off in Arlington, the heroes stirred
And meditated on the message of that bird.

*

9

And sang—oh, merciless!—to me,
Who to that place
And to that massive hour had moved, and now
Rose,
Rose naked, and shivered in moonlight, and cried
Out in my need
To know what postulate of joy men have tried
To live by, in sunlight and moonlight, until they died.

V I I Dragon-Tree

The faucet drips all night, the plumber forgot it.
A cat, in coitu, squalls like Hell's honeymoon.
A child is sick. The doctor coughs.
Do you feel, in your heart, that life has turned out as once you expected?

Spring comes early, ice
Groans in the gorge. Water, black, swirls
Into foam like lace white in fury. The gorge boulders boom.
When you hear, in darkness, the gorge boulders boom, does your heart
                                        say, "No comment"?

Geese pass in dawn-light, and the news
From Asia is bad, and the Belgians sure mucked up
The Congo. Human flesh is yet eaten there, often uncooked.
Have you sat on a hillside at sunset and eaten the flesh of your own heart?

The world drives at you like a locomotive
In an archaic movie. It whirls off the screen,
It is on you, the iron. You hear, in that silence, your heart.
Have you thought that the headlines are only the image of your own heart?

❋

II

Some study compassion. Some, confusing
Personal pathology with the logic of history, jump
Out of windows. Some walk with God, some by rivers, at twilight.
Have you tried to just sit with the children and tell a tale ending in laughter?

Oh, tell the tale, and laugh, and let
God laugh—for your heart is the dragon-tree, the root
Feels, in earth-dark, the abrasive scale, the coils
Twitch. But look! the new leaf flaps gilt in the sunlight. Birds sing.

V I I I   Vision Under the October Mountain: A Love Poem

Golding from green, gorgeous the mountain
high hangs in gold air, how
can stone float, it is

the image of authority, of reality—oh, is it?—floating
with no weight, and glows, did we
once in the womb dream, dream
a gold mountain in gold
air floating, we in the

pulse and warm slosh of
that unbreathing bouillon, lulled in
the sway of that sweet
syllogism—oh, unambiguous—swung
in the tide of that bliss unbreathed, bathed in
un-self which was self, did we
dream a gold mountain, did
it glow in that faceless unfatuous
dark, did
it glow in gold air in the airless
abstraction of dark, floating high
above our blind eyes with

*

no lashes yet, unbrined by grief yet, we
saw nothing, but
what did we dream, a
gold mountain,
floating?

I want to understand the miracle
of your presence here by my side, your
gaze on the mountain. I want

to hear the whole story of how
you came here, with
particular emphasis on the development of

the human scheme of values.

I X   Chain Saw at Dawn in Vermont in Time of Drouth

1

Dawn and, distant, the steel-snarl and lyric
Of the chain saw in deep woods:
I wake. Was it
Trunk-scream, bough-rip and swish, then earth-thud?
It is only the saw's song, the saw
Sings: *now!* Sings:
Now, now, now, in the
Blood-lust and lash of an eternal present, the present
Murders the past, the nerve shrieks, the saw

Sings *now,* and I wake, rising
From that darkness of sleep which
Is the past, and is
The self. It is
Myself, and I know how,
Now far off,
New light gilds the spruce-tops.
The saw, for a moment, ceases, and under
Arm-pits of the blue-shirted sawyer sweat
Beads cold, and
In the obscene silence of the saw's cessation,
A crow, somewhere, calls.

The crow, in distance, calls with the crystalline beauty
Of the outraged heart.

Have I learned how to live?

2

On the other side of the woods, in the village, a man
Is dying. Wakes
In dawn to the saw's song, thinks
How his wife was a good wife, wonders
Why his boy turned out bad, wonders why
He himself never managed to pay off the mortgage, thinks
Of dawn and the first light spangling the spruces, and how
He leaned on the saw and the saw
Sang. But had not known what
The saw sang. So now thinks:
I have not learned how to die, but

For that thought has no language, has only
The saw's song, in distance: glee of steel and the
Sun-shriek, the scream of castration, the whirl-tooth hysteria
Of *now, now, now!* So
Sweats. What

Can I tell him? I
Cannot tell him how to die because
I have not learned how to live—what man
Has learned how to live?—and I lie

*

In the dawn, and the thin sheet of summer
Lies on me, and I close my eyes, for
The saw sings, and I know
That soon I must rise and go out in the world where
The heel of the sun's foot smites horridly the hill,
And the stalk of the beech leaf goes limp,
And the bright brook goes gray among boulders,
And the saw sings, for

I must endeavor to learn what
I must learn before I must learn
The other thing. If
I learn even a little, I may,
By evening, be able
To tell the man something.

Or he himself may have learned by then.

X Ways of Day

I have come all this way.
I am sitting in the shade.
Book on knee and mind on nothing,
I now fix my gaze
On my small son playing in the afternoon's blaze.

Convulsive and cantankerous,
Night heaved, and burning, the star
Fell. Oh, what do I remember?
I heard the swamp owl, night-long, call.
The far car's headlight swept the room wall.

I am the dark and tricky one.
I am watching from my shade.
Your tousled hair-tips prickle the sunlight.
I watch you at your sunlit play.
Teach me, my son, the ways of day.

TALE OF TIME

I   What Happened

It was October. It was the Depression. Money
Was tight. Hoover was not a bad
Man, and my mother
Died, and God
Kept on, and keeps on,
Trying to tie things together, but

It doesn't always work, and we put the body
Into the ground, dark
Fell soon, but not yet, and oh,
Have you seen the last oak leaf of autumn, high,
Not yet fallen, stung
By last sun to a gold
Painful beyond the pain one can ordinarily
Get? What

Was there in the interim
To do, the time being the time
Between the clod's *chunk* and
The full realization, which commonly comes only after
Midnight? That
*

Is when you will go to the bathroom for a drink of water.
You wash your face in cold water.
You stare at your face in the mirror, wondering
Why now no tears come, for
You had been proud of your tears, and so
You think of copulation, of
Fluid ejected, of
Water deeper than daylight, of
The sun-dappled dark of deep woods and
Blood on green fern frond, of
The shedding of blood, and you will doubt
The significance of your own experience. Oh,
Desolation—oh, if
You were rich!
You try to think of a new position. Is this

Grief? You pray
To God that this be grief, for
You want to grieve.

This, you reflect, is no doubt the typical syndrome.

But all this will come later.
There will also be the dream of the eating of human flesh.

I I The Mad Druggist

I come back to try to remember the faces she saw every day.
She saw them on the street, at school, in the stores, at church.
They are not here now, they have been withdrawn, are put away.
They are all gone now, and have left me in the lurch.

I am in the lurch because they were part of her.
Not clearly remembering them, I have therefore lost that much
Of her, and if I do remember,
I remember the lineaments only beyond the ice-blur and soot-smutch

Of boyhood contempt, for I had not thought they were real.
The real began where the last concrete walk gave out
And the smart-weed crawled in the cracks, where the last privy canted to spill
Over flat in the rank-nourished burdock, and would soon, no doubt,

If nobody came to prop it, which nobody would do.
The real began there: field and woods, stone and stream began
Their utterance, and the fox, in his earth, knew
Joy; and the hawk, like philosophy, hung without motion, high,
                                                  where the sun-blaze of wind ran.

Now, far from Kentucky, planes pass in the night, I hear them and all, all is real.
Some men are mad, but I know that delusion may be one name for truth.
The faces I cannot remember lean at my bed-foot, and grin fit to kill,
For we now share a knowledge I did not have in my youth.

∗

There's one I remember, the old druggist they carried away.
They put him in Hoptown, where he kept on making his list—
The same list he had on the street when he stopped my mother to say:
"Here they are, Miss Ruth, the folks that wouldn't be missed,

"Or this God-durn town would be lucky to miss,
If when I fixed a prescription I just happened to pour
Something in by way of improvement." Then leaned in that gray way of his:
"But you—you always say something nice when you come in my store."

In Hoptown he worked on his list, which now could have nothing to do
With the schedule of deaths continuing relentlessly,
To include, in the end, my mother, as well as that list-maker who
Had the wit to see that she was too precious to die:

A fact some in the street had not grasped—nor the attending physician,

nor God, nor I.

I I I   Answer Yes or No

Death is only a technical correction of the market.
Death is only the transfer of energy to a new form.
Death is only the fulfilment of a wish.

Whose wish?

I V   The Interim

1

Between the clod and the midnight
The time was.
There had been the public ritual and there would be
The private realization,
And now the time was, and

In that time the heart cries out for coherence.
Between the beginning and the end, we must learn
The nature of being, in order
In the end to be, so

Our feet, in first dusk, took
Us over the railroad tracks, where
Sole-leather ground drily against cinders, as when
Tears will not come. She

Whom we now sought was old. Was
Sick. Was dying. Was
Black. Was.
Was: and was that enough? Is
Existence the adequate and only target
For the total reverence of the heart?

*

We would see her who,
Also, had held me in her arms.
She had held me in her arms,
And I had cried out in the wide
Day-blaze of the world. But

Now was a time of endings.

What is love?

2

Tell me what love is, for
The harvest moon, gold, heaved
Over the far woods which were,
On the black land black, and it swagged over
The hill-line. That light
Lay gold on the roofs of Squigg-town, and the niggers
Were under the roofs, and
The room smelled of urine.
A fire burned on the hearth:
Too hot, and there was no ventilation, and

You have not answered my question.

3

Propped in a chair, lying down she
Could not have breathed, dying
Erect, breath
Slow from the hole of the mouth, that black
Aperture in the blackness which
Was her face, but
How few of them are really
Black, but she
Is black, and life
Spinning out, spilling out, from
The holes of the eyes: and the eyes are
Burning mud beneath a sky of nothing.
The eyes bubble like hot mud with the expulsion of vision.

I lean, I am the
Nothingness which she
Sees.

Her hand rises in the air.
It rises like revelation.
It moves but has no motion, and
Around it the world flows like a dream of drowning.
The hand touches my cheek.
The voice says: *you*.

I am myself.

The hand has brought me the gift of myself.

4

I am myself, and
Her face is black like cave-blackness, and over
That blackness now hangs death, gray
Like cobweb over the blackness of a cave, but
That blackness which she is, is
Not deficiency like cave-blackness, but is
Substance.
The cobweb shakes with the motion of her breath.

My hand reaches out to part that grayness of cobweb.

My lips touch the cheek, which is black.
I do not know whether the cheek is cold or hot, but I
Know that
The temperature is shocking.
I press my lips firmly against that death,
I try to pray.

The flesh is dry, and tastes of salt.

My father has laid a twenty-dollar bill on the table.
He, too, will kiss that cheek.

5

We stand in the street of Squigg-town.
The moon is high now and the tin roofs gleam.
My brother says: *The whole place smelled of urine.*
My father says: *Twenty dollars—oh, God, what*
Is twenty dollars when
The world is the world it is!

The night freight is passing.
The couplings clank in the moonlight, the locomotive
Labors on the grade.
The freight disappears beyond the coal chute westward, and
The red caboose light disappears into the distance of the continent.
It will move all night into distance.

My sister is weeping under the sky.
The sky is enormous in the absoluteness of moonlight.

These are factors to be considered in making any final estimate.

6

There is only one solution. If
You would know how to live, here
Is the solution, and under
My window, when ice breaks, the boulder
Groans in the gorge, the foam swirls, and in
The intensity of the innermost darkness of steel
The crystal blooms like a star, and at
Dawn I have seen the delicate print of the coon-hand in silt by the riffle.

Hawk-shadow sweetly sweeps the grain.
I would compare it with that fugitive thought which I can find no word for.

7

Planes pass in the night. I turn
To the right side if the beating
Of my own heart disturbs me.
The sound of water flowing is
An image of Time, and therefore
Truth is all and
Must be respected, and
On the other side of the mirror into which,
At morning, you will stare, History

Gathers, condenses, crouches, breathes, waits. History
Stares forth at you through the eyes which
You think are the reflection of
Your own eyes in the mirror.
Ah, Monsieur du Miroir!

Your whole position must be reconsidered.

8

But the solution: You
Must eat the dead.
You must eat them completely, bone, blood, flesh, gristle, even
Such hair as can be forced. You
Must undertake this in the dark of the moon, but
At your plenilune of anguish.

Immortality is not impossible,
Even joy.

V What Were You Thinking, Dear Mother?

What were you thinking, a child, when you lay,
At the whippoorwill hour, lost in the long grass,
As sun, beyond the dark cedars, sank?
You went to the house. The lamps were now lit.

What did you think when the evening dove mourned,
Far off in those sober recesses of cedar?
What relevance did your heart find in that sound?
In lamplight, your father's head bent at his book.

What did you think when the last saffron
Of sunset faded beyond the dark cedars,
And on noble blue now the evening star hung?
You found it necessary to go to the house,

And found it necessary to live on,
In your bravery and in your joyous secret,
Into our present maniacal century,
In which you gave me birth, and in

Which I, in the public and private mania,
Have lived, but remember that once I,
A child, in the grass of that same spot, lay,
And the whippoorwill called, beyond the dark cedars.

V I Insomnia

1

If to that place. Place of grass.
If to hour of whippoorwill, I.
If I now, not a child. To.
If now I, not a child, should come to
That place, lie in
That place, in that hour hear
That call, would
I rise,
Go?

Yes, enter the darkness. Of.
Darkness of cedars, thinking
You there, you having entered, sly,
My back being turned, face
Averted, or
Eyes shut, for
A man cannot keep his eyes steadily open
Sixty years.

I did not see you when you went away.
*

Darkness of cedars, yes, entering, but what
Face, what
Bubble on dark stream of Time, white
Glimmer un-mooned? Oh,
What age has the soul, what
Face does it wear, or would
I meet that face that last I saw on the pillow, pale?

I recall each item with remarkable precision.

Would the sweat now be dried on the temples?

2

What would we talk about? The dead,
Do they know all, or nothing, and
If nothing, does
Curiosity survive the long unravelment? Tell me

What they think about love, for I
Know now at long last that the living remember the dead only
Because we cannot bear the thought that they
Might forget us. Or is
That true? Look, look at these—
But no, no light here penetrates by which
You might see these photographs I keep in my wallet. Anyway,
I shall try to tell you all that has happened to me.

Though how can I tell when I do not even know?

And as for you, and all the interesting things
That must have happened to you and that
I am just dying to hear about—

But would you confide in a balding stranger
The intimate secret of death?

3

Or does the soul have many faces, and would I,
Pacing the cold hypothesis of Time, enter
Those recesses to see, white,
Whiter than moth-wing, the child's face
Glimmer in cedar gloom, and so
Reach out that I might offer
What protection I could, saying,
"I am older than you will ever be"—for it
Is the child who once
Lay lost in the long grass, sun setting.

Reach out, saying: "Your hand—
Give it here, for it's dark and, my dear,
You should never have come in the woods when it's dark,
But I'll take you back home, they're waiting."
And to woods-edge we come, there stand.

I watch you move across the open space.
You move under the paleness of new stars.
You move toward the house, and one instant,

A door opening, I see
Your small form black against the light, and the door
Is closed, and I

✻

Hear night crash down a million stairs.
In the ensuing silence
My breath is difficult.

Heat lightning ranges beyond the horizon.

That, also, is worth mentioning.

4

Come,
Crack crust, striker
From darkness, and let seize—let what
Hand seize, oh!—my heart, and compress
The heart till, after pain, joy from it
Spurt like a grape, and I will grind
Teeth on flint tongue till
The flint screams. Truth
Is all. But

I must learn to speak it
Slowly, in a whisper.

Truth, in the end, can never be spoken aloud,
For the future is always unpredictable.
But so is the past, therefore

At wood's edge I stand, and,
Over the black horizon, heat lightning
Ripples the black sky. After
The lightning, as the eye
Adjusts to the new dark,
The stars are, again, born.

They are born one by one.

HOMAGE TO EMERSON,
ON NIGHT FLIGHT TO NEW YORK

TO PETER AND EBIE BLUME

I   His Smile

Over Peoria we lost the sun:
The earth, by snow like sputum smeared, slides
Westward. Those fields in the last light gleam. Emerson—

The essays, on my lap, lie. A finger
Of light, in our pressurized gloom, strikes down,
Like God, to poke the page, the page glows. There is
No sin. Not even error. Night,

On the glass at my right shoulder, hisses
Like sand from a sand-blast, but
The hiss is a sound that only a dog's
Ear could catch, or the human heart. My heart

Is as abstract as an empty
Coca-Cola bottle. It whistles with speed.
It whines in that ammoniac blast caused by
The passage of stars, for
At 38,000 feet Emerson

Is dead right. His smile
Was sweet as he walked in the greenwood.
He walked lightly, his toes out, his body
Swaying in the dappled shade, and
His smile never withered a violet. He

*

Did not even know the violet's name, not having
Been introduced, but he bowed, smiling,
For he had forgiven God everything, even the violet.

When I was a boy I had a wart on the right forefinger.

I I The Wart

At 38,000 feet you had better
Try to remember something specific, if
You yourself want to be something specific, I remember
The wart and the old colored man, he said, *Son*
You quit that jack-off, and that thing go way,
And I said *Quit what,* and he giggled *He-he,* and he
Said, *You is got white skin and hair red as a ter-mater, but*
You is human-kind, but

At 38,000 feet that is hard to remember.

I I I   The Spider

The spider has more eyes than I have money.
I used to dream that God was a spider, or

Vice versa, but it is easier
To dream of a funnel, and you
The clear liquid being poured down it, forever.

You do not know what is beyond the little end of the funnel.

The liquid glimmers in darkness, you
Are happy, it pours easily, without fume.

All you have to do is not argue.

I V One Drunk Allegory

Not argue, unless, that is, you are the kind
That needs to remember something specific
In order to be, at 38,000 feet, whatever you are, and once
In New Orleans, in French Town, in
Front of the Old Absinthe House, and it
Was Saturday night, was 2 A.M., a drunk

Crip slipped, and the air was full of flying crutches
Like a Texas tornado exploding with chicken feathers and
Split boards off busted hen-houses, and bingo!—
It was prize money flat on its you-know-what, it
Was like a box of spilled spaghetti, but
I managed to reassemble everything and prop it

Against a lamp post. *Thank you,*
It said in its expensive Harvard-cum-cotton
Voice, then bingo!—
Flat on its you-know-what, on the pavement,
And ditto the crutches. *Prithee,* the voice

Expensively said, *do not trouble yourself*
Further. This is as good a position as any
From which to watch the stars. Then added:
Until, of course, the cops come. I
Had private reasons for not wanting to be
There when the cops came. So wasn't.

✻

44

Emerson thought that significance shines through everything,

And at that moment I was drunk enough to think all this was allegory.
If it was, it was sure-God one drunk allegory, and
Somewhere in the womb-gloom of the DC-8

A baby is crying. The cry seems to have a reality
Independent of the baby. The cry
Is like a small white worm in my brain.

It nibbles with tiny, insistent assiduity. Its teeth
Are almost too soft. Sometimes it merely tickles.

To my right, far over Kentucky, the stars are shining.

V Multiplication Table

If the Christmas tree at Rockefeller Center were
A billion times bigger, and you laid it
Flat down in the dark, and
With a steam roller waist-high to God and heavy as
The Rocky Mountains, flattened it out thin as paper, but
Never broke a single damned colored light bulb, and they were all
Blazing in the dark, that would be the way it is, but

Beyond the lights it is dark, and one night in winter, I
Stood at the end of a pier at Coney Island, while
The empty darkness howled like a dog, but no wind, and far down
The boardwalk what must have been a cop's flashlight
Jiggled fitfully over what must have been locked store-fronts, then,
Of a sudden, went out. The stars were small and white, and I heard

The sea secretly sucking the piles of the pier with a sound like
An old woman sucking her teeth in the dark before she sleeps.

The nose of the DC-8 dips, and at this point
The man sitting beside me begins, quite audibly, to recite
The multiplication table.

                    Far below,
Individual lights can be seen throbbing like nerve ends.
I have friends down there, and their lives have strange shapes
Like eggs splattered on the kitchen floor. Their lives shine
Like oil-slicks on dark water. I love them, I think.

In a room, somewhere, a telephone keeps ringing.

46

V I Wind

The wind comes off the Sound, smelling
Of ice. It smells
Of fish and burned gasoline. A sheet
Of newspaper drives in the wind across
The great distance of cement that bleeds
Off into blackness beyond the red flares. The air

Shivers, it shakes like Jello with
The roar of jets—oh, why
Is it you think you can hear the infinitesimal scrape
Of that newspaper as it slides over the black cement, forever?

The wind gouges its knuckles into my eye. No wonder there are tears.

V I I Does the Wild Rose?

When you reach home tonight you will see
That the envelope containing the policy
Of your flight insurance is waiting, unopened,
On the table. All had been in order,
In case—but can you tell me,

Does the wild rose know your secret
As the summer silence breathes?

Eastward, the great waters stretch in darkness.
Do you know how gulls sleep when they can't make it home?

Tell me, tell me, does the wild rose—tell me, for

Tonight I shall dream of small white stars
Falling forever in darkness like dandruff, but

Now let us cross that black cement which so resembles the arctic ice of
Our recollections. There is the city, the sky
Glows, glows above it, there must be

A way by which the process of living can become Truth.

✳

Let us move toward the city. Do you think you could tell me
What constitutes the human bond? Do you ever think
Of a face half in shadow, tears—
As it would seem from that muted glitter—in the
Eyes, but

The lips do not tremble.

Is it merely a delusion that they seem about to smile?

Shoes in Rain Jungle

Shoes rot off feet before feet
Rot, and before feet
Stop moving feet
Rot, rot in the
Rain, moving.

Napoleon was wrong, an army
Marches on its feet. If
It has them. If
The feet have shoes.

The Battle of Gettysburg was fought for shoes.
It is hell to die barefoot, unless,
Of course, that is the way you are raised.

They are cheap, but shoes are dear, and

All wars are righteous. Except when
You lose them. This
Is the lesson of history. This—
And shoes. On rotting shoe leather

Men march into history, and when
You get there take a good look around, lost
In the multitudinous gray portieres of beaded
Rain, and say, *"Mot de Cambronne,* this
Is history."

Now you know what it is.
*

History is what you can't
Resign from, but

There is always refuge in the practice
Of private virtue,
Or at least in heroism, and if

You get stuck with heroism you can, anyway,
When the cameras pop, cover your face,
Like the man who, coming out of the D. A.'s office,
Lifts his hands, handcuffed, to cover his face.

You can do that much.

Melville, ruined, sick, acerb, anent
The Civil War, said: "Nothing
Can lift the heart of man
Like manhood in a fellow-man," and

Sociologists should make a study called "Relative
Incidence of Mention of Heroes in News Media
As Index to Gravity of a Situation."

Sociologists can do that much.

And when the rainy season is over
There will be new problems, including
The problem of a new definition of virtue.

Meanwhile talk as little *mot de Cambronne* as
Possible, and remember
There is more than one kind of same.

This last is very important.

Fall Comes in Back-Country Vermont

TO WILLIAM MEREDITH

(1 One Voter Out of Sixteen)

Deader they die here, or at least
Differently, deeper the hole, and after
The burying, at night, late, you
Are more apt to wonder about the drainage

Of the cemetery, but know that you needn't, for
Here's all hills anyway, or mountain, and the hole
Standard, but if no drainage problem, yet
You may still wake with a kind of psychic

Twitch, as when the nerves in the amputee's
Stump (a saw did it, no doubt) twitch and wonder
How that which has gone off and set up
As a separate self is making out, and whether

It repents of its rashness, and would like
To come back and crawl into bed and be
Forgiven, and even though you, like me,
May forget the name of the dead, in the dark you

Can't help but remember that if there are only
Sixteen voters and one dies, that leaves only
Fifteen, and no doubt you know the story
Of how it began, how he laid his axe down, then

*

Just sat on a log, not saying a word, till
The crew knocked off for the day, and never
Came back (it was cancer), and later you'd see him
Sit on the porch in the sun and throw bread

To the chipmunks, but that was last year, and now
There's the real-estate sign in the yard, and the grass
Not cut, and already one window knocked out,
For the widow's heartbroken and gone, and the bed

Is stripped to the mattress, and the bedpan
Washed with ammonia and put on a high shelf,
And the stuffed lynx he shot now all night glares
At the empty room with a feral vindication,

And does not forgive, and thinks with glee
How cancer is worse than a 30.30, and

(2 The Bear and the Last Person to Remember)

It is well the widow is gone, for here winter's
Not made for a woman lone, lorn, and slow-foot,
And summer already sinks southward, and soon
All over the state the summer people

Will put the lawn mower in the red barn, drain
The plumbing, deny the pain of that heart-pinch
They cannot define, and get out the suitcase
To pack, for last night, in moonlight and high

*

On the mountain, I heard the first bear-hoot,
As the bear that all day had stripped bushes of the last
Blueberries, felt that hot itch and heaved
Up his black, hairy man-height in moonlight,

Lifted the head and curled back the black lip
To show the white moon-gleam of tusk, and the throat
Pulsed in that call that is like the great owl's,
But more edged with anguish, and then far off,

From a ruined orchard, by the old cellar hole,
In the tang and tawny air-taste of the apple-
Night, the she bear, too, rises,
And the half-crushed apple, forgotten, falls

From the jaw gone slack in that moment before
Her utterance, and soon now, night after night,
On the mountain the moon-air will heave with that hunger,
So that, in that hour, the boys of the village

Come out, climb a ridge and reply, and when
Off on the mountain that hoot comes, and nearer,
The girls with them shiver and giggle, not quite
Daring to face that thought that from dark now,

Hot-breathed and hairy, earth-odored and foam-flecked,
Rises, and want to go home, all but one,
Who feels that the night cannot breathe, and who soon,
On the raw mattress, in that house, will cry

*

Out, but the house is empty, and
Through the window where once the lace curtains hung
And a green shade was but is not,
The moonlight now pours like God, and the sweat

Of her effort goes ice, for she remembers,
So struggles to thrust off that weight that chokes her,
Thrusts herself up on that mattress, and gasping
In that ice and ice-iron of moonlight, with

What breath in that dishevelment
Is possible, says: "But here—it was here—
On this bed that he died, and I'll catch it and die"—
But does not, comes back, comes back until snow flies,

And many years later will be the last person
To remember his name who there on that bed

(3 The Human Fabric)

Had died, but for now let us take some comfort
In the fact that the fifteen surviving voters,
Remembering his name, feel, in the heart,
Diminished, for in this section death

Is a window gone dark and a face not seen
Any more at the P. O., and in the act
Of rending irreparably the human fabric,
Death affirms the fact of that fabric, so what
*

55

If at night, in first snow, the hunters pass—
Pale clerks and mechanics from Springfield and Hartford
With red caps and rifles and their pitiful
Blood-lust and histrionic maleness—and passing,

Throw out from the car the empty bourbon
Bottle to lie in the snow by the For-
Sale sign, and snow covers the bottle, will cover
The sign itself, and then the snow plow

Will pile up the banks as high as the eaves,
So that skiers who sing past in sports cars at dusk
Cannot see it, nor singing, need yet to know
The truth which at last they will come to need,

That life is of life paradigm, and death
The legend of death, nor need ever to know

(4 Afterwards)

That all night, eaves-high, the snow will press
Its face to the black ice of glass, and by
The white light its own being sheds, stare
Into that trapped cubicle of emptiness which

Is that room, but by that time I
Will not be here, in another place be,
And in my bed, not asleep, will endeavor
To see in my mind the eagle that once,
*

Above sunset, above the mountain in Stratton,
I saw—on thinnest air, high, saw
Lounging—oh, look!—it turns, and turning,
Shoulders like spray that last light before

The whistling down-plunge to the mountain's shade.
I touch the hand there on the pillow.

THE DAY DR. KNOX DID IT

TO WILLIAM AND ROSE STYRON

I   Place and Time

Heat-blaze, white dazzle: and white is the dust
down the only street of Cerulean Springs,
which is only a piece of country road
mislaid, somehow, among the white houses,

as the houses, too, had got mislaid
among the last big oaks and big tulip trees left
from the old forest-time. But to resume:
heat-dazzle, dust-whiteness—an image in sleep,

or in the brain behind the eyeball,
as now, in the light of this other day,
and year, the eyeball, stunned by that inner
blaze, sees nothing, can nothing see

outward whatsoever—only
the white dust of that street, and it
is always August, is 3 P.M.,
the mercury 95, and the leaf

of the oak tree curls at the edge like leather,
and the post master's setter pants in his cave
of cool back under the rotting floor boards
of the P. O.'s high old porch, and every

*

shade is down in every house,
and the last ash winks in the black kitchen range,
and the iron creaks with contraction in the lonely
new silence of the kitchen. Far off,

when the head of the moccasin parts the green
algae and it slides up out of the slough,
its trail on the stone sizzles dry in a twinkling,
and the lunacy of the cicada knows

now no remission. The sun is white.
It fills the sky with a scream of whiteness,
and my feet move in the white dust.
My feet are bare, I am nine years old,

and my feet in the white dust move, but I move
in a dream that is silver like willow and water
and the glimmer of water on water-dark stone.
I see in my mind that place I will go.

This is the summer of 1914.
I move toward that coolness. Then I hear the sound.

I I The Event

The sound was like one made by a board
dropped from a builder's scaffold to fall
flat and heavy on another
board grounded solid and flat to make

the sound solid. But cottony, too,
as though its own echoes were tangled in it,
in thickness and softness—an effect that was caused,
no doubt, by the fact he had climbed to the barn loft

to arrange himself. That summer I'd played
there in that loft, and so knew how
if you lay on your back in the hay, all
you could see was the twilight of spider-web

hung from the rooftree, or maybe one wasp
cruising slow in that gloom with one
sharp glint of light on his hard sheen.
That man—how long had he lain, just looking?

That was the thing that stuck in my head.
I would wonder how long he had lain there, first.

I I I   A Confederate Veteran Tries to Explain the Event

"But why did he do it, Grandpa?" I said
to the old man sitting under the cedar,
who had come a long way to that place, and that time
when that other man lay down in the hay

to arrange himself. And now the old man
lifted his head to stare at me.
"It's one of those things," he said, and stopped.
"What things?" I said. And he said: "Son—

"son, one of those things you never know."
"But there must be a *why,*" I said. Then he
said: "Folks—yes, folks, they up and die."
"But, Grandpa—" I said. And he: "They die."

Said: "Yes, by God, and I've seen 'em die.
I've seen 'em die and I've seen 'em dead.
I've seen 'em die hot and seen 'em die cold.
Hot lead and cold steel—" The words, they stopped.

The mouth closed up. The eyes looked away.
Beyond the lawn where the fennel throve,
beyond the fence where the whitewash peeled,
beyond the cedars along the lane,

the eyes fixed. The land, in sunlight,
swam, with the meadow the color of rust,
and distance the blue of Time, and nothing—
oh, nothing—would ever happen, and

*

in the silence my breath did not happen. But
the eyes, they happened, they found me, I
stood there and waited. "Dying," he said,
"hell, dying's a thing any fool can do."

"But what made him do it?" I said, again.
Then wished I hadn't, for he stared at me.
He stared at me as though I weren't there,
or as though I were dead, or had never been born,

and I felt like dandelion fuzz blown away,
or a word you'd once heard but never could spell,
or only an empty hole in the air.
From the cedar shade his eyes burned red.

Darker than shade, his mouth opened then.
Spit was pink on his lips, I saw the tongue move
beyond the old teeth, in the dark of his head.
It moved in that dark. Then, "Son—" the tongue said.

"For some folks the world gets too much," it said.
In that dark, the tongue moved. "For some folks," it said.

I V The Place Where the Boy Pointed

It was ten days after the event
when the son of the man who had lain in the hay
took me back to the loft where we'd once played,
but this time it wasn't to play, though for what

I didn't know, he just said, "Come on,"
and when I came, and there we stood
in the spider-web gloom and wasp-glint light,
he stood, his face white in shadow, and pointed.

I stared at the place, but the hay was clean,
which was strange, for I'd been hearing them tell
how a 12-gauge will make an awful mess
if you put the muzzle in your mouth.

I kept thinking about how the place looked clean.
I kept wondering who had cleaned up the mess.

V   And All That Came Thereafter

But ran from such wondering as I ran
down the street, and the street was dancing a-dazzle,
and the dust rose white in plops round my feet
as they ran toward that stream that was silent and silver

in willow and water, and I would lie
with my eyes shut tight, and let water flow
over me as I lay, and like water, the world
would flow, flow away, on forever. But once

in San Francisco, on Telegraph Hill,
past midnight, alone, and that was
in the time long before that imbecile
tower had there been built, and there I

watched fog swell up from the sea and lean,
and star by star blot the sky out,
and blot the hill, and blot me out
from all relation but to the dry

goat droppings that beneath my feet
pressed the thin soles of my sneakers, as I,
in that swirl of whiteness gone blinder than black,
lifted up my arms, and while distantly

I heard the freighter, savage in fog,
slide past the passage of the Gate,
my own heart, in a rage like joy,
burst. I did not know my name,

*

nor do I know, even now, the meaning
of another night, by another sea,
when sea-salt on the laurel leaf
in moonlight, like frost, gleamed, and salt

were the tears to my lips on the girl's face, for
she wept, and I did not know why, and thus
entered her body, and in that breathless
instant of poised energy, heard

the sea-sway and the secret grind
of shingle down the glimmering shore.
Later, we lay and heard it. It
from the hollow of earth seemed, but the moon

hung steady as eternity. Now
I sometimes cannot remember her face, nor
the name of the village where we had stayed,
and as for Telegraph Hill, long since

gone is the immigrant's goat, and there now
wearers of pin-stripe and of furs by I. Magnin
have swarmed in their hives of glass to admire
from that point of vantage the rising values

of real estate and the beauty of stars,
which yet in fact shine, and if there is fog,
high above the last gray unravelment, shine,
while fog-wrapped, the freighters, and troopships now **too,**

seaward slide, and hooting, proceed
in darkness, and deeper in darkness blooms
the inward orchid, and agon, blind,
of this, our age, of which I—who

*

have lied, in velleity loved, in weakness
forgiven, who have stolen small objects, committed
adultery, and for a passing pleasure,
as well as for reasons of sanitation,

inflicted death on flies—am,
like you, the perfect image, and if
once through the blaze of that August I fled,
but toward myself I fled, for there is

no water to wash the world away.
We are the world, and it is too late
to pretend we are children at dusk watching fireflies.
But we must frame more firmly the idea of good.

My small daughter's dog has been killed on the road.
It is night. In the next room she weeps.

HOLY WRIT

TO VANN AND GLENN WOODWARD

I   Elijah on Mount Carmel

(Elijah, after the miraculous fall of fire on his altar, the breaking of the drouth, and the slaughter of the priests of Baal, girds up his loins and runs ahead of the chariot of Ahab to the gates of Jezreel, where Jezebel waits.)

Nothing is re-enacted. Nothing
Is true. Therefore nothing
Must be believed,
But
To have truth
Something must be believed,
And repetition and congruence,
To say the least, are necessary, and
His thorn-scarred heels and toes with filth horn-sealed
Spurned now the flint-edge and with blood spurts flailed
Stone, splashed mud of Jezreel. And he screamed.
He had seen glory more blood-laced than any he had dreamed.

Far, far ahead of the chariot tire,
Which the black mud sucked, he screamed,
Screaming in glory
Like
A bursting blood blister.
Ahead of the mud-faltered fetlock,
He screamed, and of Ahab huddled in
The frail vehicle under the purpling wrack
And spilled gold of storm—poor Ahab, who,
From metaphysical confusion and lightning, had nothing to run to
But the soft Phoenician belly and commercial acuity
Of Jezebel: that darkness wherein History creeps to die.

*

How could he ever tell her? Get nerve to?
Tell how around her high altar
The prinking and primped
Priests,
Limping, had mewed,
And only the gull-mew was answer,
No fire to heaped meats, only sun-flame,
And the hairy one laughed: "Has your god turned aside to make pee-pee?"
How then on that sea-cliff he prayed, fire fell, sky darkened,
Rain fell, drouth broke now, for God had hearkened,
And priests gave their death-squeal. The king hid his eyes in his coat.
Oh, why to that hairy one should God have hearkened, who smelled like a goat?

Yes, how could he tell her? When he himself
Now scarcely believed it? Soon,
In the scented chamber,
She,
Saying, "Baby, Baby,
Just hush, now hush, it's all right,"
Would lean, reach out, lay a finger
To his lips to allay his infatuate gabble. So,
Eyes shut, breath scant, he heard her breath rip the lamp-flame
To blackness, and by that sweet dog-bait, lay, and it came,
The soft hand-grope he knew he could not, nor wished to, resist
Much longer; so prayed: "Dear God, dear God—oh, please, don't exist!"

I I Saul at Gilboa

(Samuel Speaks)

1

From landscape the color of lions.
From land of great stone the color,
At noon-blaze, of the droppings of lions,
But harder than iron and,
By moonlight, bone-white, and the crouched stone seizes,
In its teeth, the night-wind, and the wind
Yelps, the wind
Yowls. From
The district of dry thorn, the ankle
Scarred by thorn. From
The dry watercourses.
Came.

He had been seeking his father's lost asses.

Sought what he found not, but found
Me, for what
We seek we never
Find, find only fate. Which is,
Not the leaf, but the shadow
Of the leaf, turning in air.

Fate is the air we breathe.

He moved toward me, and in that motion
His body clove the bright air.

69

2

How beautiful are the young, walking
On the fore-part of the foot, the hair of the head,
Without ointment, glistens, the lower
Lip, though the fat of burnt meat has long since
Been wiped, glistens, and
Eyes with the glister of vision like
The eyes, hunger-whetted, of the eagle
That from the high sky stares.

His hands, by his sides, heavy hang down like hammers.

(Let Amalek shiver in his tent of goat hair.
Let him put belly to belly and no cloth between, not waiting
For the hour when stars, in blackness, are burnished by
The cold wind.)

Toward me he walks, I am old.
Dust of desert on him, and thorn-scar, he
Walks, and is the man. He is,
From the shoulder and upward, higher than any among the people.
*

He comes walking who will make Israel
One among the nations. He walks
In his youth, which is the sweet affront
Of ignorance, toward me, and I
Smile, feeling my face, even in that smile, go stiff as
Fresh goat hide, unflayed, set in sun, goes,
For the people murmur, say
I am old. A king
They would have, and toward me
He walks who will make all things
New. In beauty toward
My knowledge, walks. What
Is in my heart?

I hear my own voice. It says: *My son.*

3

Before the knowledge in me, he, beautiful, down in the dirt, kneels.
Desert-travel and dry sweat: his odor
Is like old curds and new wine, and it comes to my nostrils.
His head is bowed, and I see the twin plaitings of muscle
At the back of his neck, and how they are grappled,
Olive root in rock, in shoulder-flesh. They grapple
To great bone, new sweat now
Beads in the channel of the back of his neck below
The skull, the skull is a tower of brass
Bent before me. He
Is ignorant, and I pour
Oil on those locks that no new shining need.

The far hills, white light on gypsum, dazzle.
The hills waver like salt dissolving in water. Swim
In the dazzle of my eyes.

4

I am the past time, am old, but
Am, too, the time to come, for I,
In my knowledge, close my eyes, and am
The membrane between the past and the future, am thin, and
That thinness is the present time, the membrane
Is only my anguish, through which
The past seeps, penetrates, is absorbed into
The future, through which
The future bleeds into, becomes, the past even before
It ceases to be
The future. Am also

The knife edge that divides.

I say to him that the asses of his father that were lost
Are found.

Say to him that at Tabor at
A high place a band of the prophets,
With psaltery and tabret, dancing, will come,
And into him will enter that breath which
Will make him dance.
He will be another man.

Before me, his head is bowed. The oil glistens.

*

Say he will dance, but I do not say
That that dance is a dance into self-hood—and oh!
Beautiful is ignorance kneeling—and do not
Say how black, when the dance-breath goes out, will be
The blackness, nor say how the young boy
Before him will sit, and strike the harp,
Nor how he at him, because he is young
And the brow smooth, will hurl
The great spear, and the boy will, like smoke, sway,
Slip from his presence, be gone, his foot
Leaving no print among rocks.

He himself will become a friend to darkness, be counseled by wolves.

5

I do not say that I will anoint against him that boy
Of the smooth brow.

Nor say how, at the hour
When the hosts are gathered, he will,
To Endor, in a mantle not his own,
In dark, come. Enter,
And to the woman of the cave speak, for, in the end,
To know is, always, all. To know
Is, whatever the knowledge, the secret hope within
Hope. So to the cave.

And from death, I,
In shape of shadow, rise,
Stand. He bows down
Before me, and in the fierceness of last joy, I see
That the hair of his bent head is
Now streaked with gray, so say
That the breath of the dance which has passed from him will not
Return. In the dirt,

He falls down.

6

The woman, who had cried out, "O thou
Art Saul!" and whose life he held in his hand—
She lifts him, gives him to eat.
She feeds him, morsel
By morsel, he like a child.
His jaws move in the labor of grinding by which life is, but
His eyes are in the distance of
Knowledge. He goes

From the cave. But not before
He has cast down the ring, massy of gold, beside her
Who now lies stretched out, eyes closed, face pressed to earth.

She has not stirred. In the silence my voice says:
"Take it, for it
Is of a man who was once a
King." The clink
Of armor, on stone, muted,
From distance and dark outside, comes,
Ceases. "A king," my voice says, "but
Now goes to be

Himself."

7

I had once poured oil on his head.

It had been in sun-blaze, at
The hour of minimal shadow,
And what shadow fell, fell
Black on stone that swam
White with light.

The cicada was hushed.

He kissed the backs of my hands, rose,
Stood, and was ashamed
Before me, who needs must look upward to his face,
Of his tallness.

The toes of his inordinate sandals
Turned inward somewhat, like
A boy. Of the left foot,
Of the great toe, the nail
Was blackened. Bruised,
In the desert, by stone.

I saw it.
*

He moved from me in the white light.
The black dwindle in distance which now he
Was, was upheld by
White light as by
A hand. He moved across distance, as across
The broad hand of my knowing.
The palm of my hand was as
Wide as the world and the
Blaze of distance. The fingers
Of my hand itched.

How beautiful are the young, walking!

I closed my eyes. I shuddered in a rage of joy.

8

The south shoulder of the pass:
And first light, gray, on the right hand,
Came. Not light. Grayness
Not strong enough to cast shadow.

Before redness sudden on east rim, before
The sudden awareness of shadows individual
From eastward, cast by
The random of hunched stones, a stallion,
Far off, neighed, once. I see,
In the shadow of imagination, the beast, dim, large,
Gray as stone. That host
From the shadowy inwardness of which
Then, a brazen *blat* from horn-throat came,
Lower lay, and westwards.

Gilboa is, of that place, the name. There,
With his son whom the sly harpist had loved
With a love surpassing the love of women,
He died. The great torso, a stake
Thrust upward to twist the gut-tangle, towered
Above the wall of Beth-shan, but
With no authority, ha! For the head

Lies at Gilboa. The sky
Is above it, and
The ant has entered
The eye-arch.

9

The death I have entered is a death
In which I cannot lie down.

I have forgotten, literally, God, and through
The enormous hollow of my head, History
Whistles like a wind.

How beautiful are the young, walking!

If I could weep.

DELIGHT

I Into Broad Daylight

Out of silence walks delight.
   Delight comes on soundless foot
Into the silence of night,
Or into broad daylight.

Delight comes like surprise.
   Delight will prepare you never.
Delight waits beyond range of your eyes
Till the moment of surprise.

Delight knows its own reason,
   A reason you will never know.
Your will, nor hand, can never seize on
Delight. Delight knows its season.

I have met delight at dawn-crest.
   I have met delight at dove-fall
When sunset reddens the dove's breast.
I may not divulge the rest:

Nor can it be guessed.

I I Love: Two Vignettes

1 Mediterranean Beach, Day after Storm

How instant joy, how clang
And whang the sun, how
Whoop the sea, and oh,
Sun, sing, as whiter than
Rage of snow, let sea the spume
Fling.

Let sea the spume, white, fling,
White on blue wild
With wind, let sun
Sing, while the world
Scuds, clouds boom and belly,
Creak like sails, whiter than,
Brighter than,
Spume in sun-song, oho!
The wind is bright.

Wind the heart winds
In constant coil, turning
In the—forever—light.

Give me your hand.

2 Deciduous Spring

Now, now, the world
All gabbles joy like geese, for
An idiot glory the sky
Bangs. Look!
All leaves are new, are
Now, are
Bangles dangling and
Spangling, in sudden air
Wangling, then
Hanging quiet, bright.

The world comes back, and again
Is gabbling, and yes,
Remarkably worse, for
The world is a whirl of
Green mirrors gone wild with
Deceit, and the world
Whirls green on a string, then
The leaves go quiet, wink
From their own shade, secretly.

Keep still, just a moment, leaves.

There is something I am trying to remember.

I I I   Something Is Going to Happen

Something is going to happen, I tell you I know.
This morning, I tell you, I saw ice in the bucket.
Something is going to happen and you can't duck it.
The way the wind blows is the way the dead leaves go.
Something is going to happen, and I'm telling you so.

Something is going to happen, I declare it.
It always happens on days like this, Mother said.
No, I didn't make the world, or make apples red,
But if you're a man you'll buck up and try to bear it.
For this morning the sun rose in the east, I swear it.

Something is going to happen, I swear it will.
Men have wept watching water flow,
And feet move fastest down the old track they know.
Look, look!—how light is lying across that hill!
Something may happen today if you don't sit still.

Something is going to happen without a doubt.
If you aren't careful it may happen this very minute.
Have you ever looked in a drawer and found nothing in it?
Have you ever opened your mouth and tried to shout,
But something happened and the shout would not come out?

✳

Something is going to happen whatever you say.
Whether you look out the window or walk in the door
Some things will be less, and other things more.
It's simply no use to turn your head away.
Something is bound to happen on a day like today

To change everything any-which-a-way,
For the sound of your name is only a mouthful of air
And the lost and the found may be found or lost anywhere.
Therefore to prepare you there's one more thing I must say:
Delight may dawn, as the day dawned, calmly, today.

I V Dream of a Dream the Small Boy Had

All night the small boy kept climbing the tree.
Sleep was the tree. The darkness roared like wind.
Oh, didn't you know that the wind is round, like a ball?
It goes round and round, like going somewhere, but is here.
It goes away and away, but is here, and you hear it.
So I said, *Oh, wind, go away,* and it did, in the dark.

But I didn't know where the wind went, which was bad,
For I was bright-colored like leaves in the blow-away time,
And wind blew me away, I didn't know where, where I was,
And maybe I wasn't, for the colors were gone,
And I dream of the tree in the dark, and no wind,
And the silence swells up to the stars, and the stars
Gasp like fish in a basket, and there is no light, and my bones,
They hang in the tree, shaped like me, and they burn.
Like fireflies or witchwood or foxfire, they shine in the dark,
Or like old kitchen matches gone damp and left in the dark.

Wind has blown me away, all but my bright bones,
Which maybe weren't me to begin with, but only my secret,
And it's awful to have your secret on fire in the dark,
Or maybe there wasn't a secret, just the lie the wind told.
Where I am I don't know now, but hear my own heart
Off somewhere singing. Where? If only I had
My geography book I could do my lesson and find
Where the Andes are and my heart a bird singing.
It must be singing in the high, bright snow, or maybe Asia.

It sings in a foreign language, like pig-latin, or joy.

V   Two Poems About Suddenly and a Rose

1   Dawn

Suddenly. Is. Now not what was *not,*
But what is. From nothing of *not*
Now all of *is.* All is. Is light, and suddenly
Dawn—and the world, in blaze of *is,*
Burns. Is flame, of time and tense
The bold combustion, and
The flame of *is,* in fury
And ungainsayable updraft of that
Black chimney of what is *not,*
Roars. Christmas—

Remember, remember!—and into flame
All those gay wrappings the children fling, then
In hands of *now,* they hold
Presents of *is,* and while
Flame leaps, they, in joy,
Scream. Oh, children,

Now to me sing, I see
Forever on the leaf the light. Snow
On the pine-leaf, against the bright blue
Forever of my mind, like breath,
Balances. Light,

*

Suddenly, on any morning, is, and somewhere,
In a garden you will never
See, dew, in fracture of light
And lunacy of gleam-glory, glitters on
A petal red as blood, and

The rose dies, laughing.

2 Intuition

Suddenly, suddenly, everything
Happens, it seems. For example, it
Rains—or it does not rain—and suddenly
Life takes on a new dimension, and old pain
Is wisdom—Christ, believe that
And you'll believe anything. But
Everything, some day, is suddenly, and life
Is what you are living, not
What you thought you had lived
All your life, but suddenly
Know you had not—oh, suddenly is what
Mother did not tell, for
How could she when
Suddenly is too sudden to tell, and

The rose dies laughing, suddenly.

V I   Not to Be Trusted

Delight is not to be trusted.
It will betray you.
Delight will undo the work of your hand
In a secret way. You

Cannot trust delight.
As I have told you,
It undoes the ambition of the young and
The wisdom of the old. You

Are not exempt. Though it yet
Has never undone you,
Look! In that bush, with wolf-fang white, delight
Humps now for someone: *You.*

V I I Finisterre

Mist drifts on the bay's face
And the last of day, it would seem, goes under,
But it's hard to tell in this northern place
If this, now, is truly the day's end, or

If, in a new shift of mist,
The light may break through yonder
To stab gold to the gray sea, and twist
Your heart to a last delight—or at least, to wonder.

From YOU, EMPERORS,
AND OTHERS
Poems *1957–1960*

GARLAND FOR YOU

I Clearly About You

Bene fac, hoc tecum feres.

—ON TOMB OF ROMAN CITIZEN OF NO
HISTORICAL IMPORTANCE, UNDER THE EMPIRE

Whoever you are, this poem is clearly about you,
For there's nothing else in the world it could be about.
Whatever it says, this poem is clearly true,
For truth is all we are born to, and the truth's out.

You won't look in the mirror? Well—but your face is there
Like a face drowned deep under water, mouth askew,
And the tongue in that mouth tastes cold water, not sweet air,
And if it could scream in that medium, the scream would be you.

Your mother preferred the more baroque positions.
Your father's legerdemain marks the vestry accounts.
So you didn't know? Well, it's time you did—though one shuns
To acknowledge the root from which one's own virtue mounts.

In the age of denture and reduced alcoholic intake,
When the crow's dawn-calling stirs memories you'd better eschew,
You will try the cross, or the couch, for balm for the heart's ache—
But that stranger who's staring so strangely, he knows you are you.

Things are getting somewhat out of hand now—light fails on the salt-flat.
In the back lot the soft-faced delinquents are whistling like snipe.
That letter—why doesn't it come!—You finger your heart that,
At a touch, in the bosom now bleeds, like a plum over-ripe.

Burn this poem, though it wring its small hands and try to jerk back.
But no use, for in bed, into your pajama pocket,
It will creep, and sleep as snug as a field mouse in haystack,
And its heart to your heart all night makes a feather-soft racket.

95

I I   The Letter About Money, Love, or Other Comfort, if Any

In the beginning was the Word.
—THE GOSPEL ACCORDING TO ST. JOHN

Having accepted the trust so many years back,
    before seven wars, nine coups d'état, and the deaths of friends and friendships,
    before having entered the world of lurkers, shirkers, burkers, tipsters and tips,
    or even discovered I had small knack
    for honesty, but only a passion, like a disease, for Truth,
    having, as I have said, accepted the trust
    those long years back in my youth,
    it's no wonder that now I admit, as I must,
    to no recollection whatever
    of wens, moles, scars, or his marks of identification—but do recall my disgust
    at the odor of garlic and a somewhat perfervid eye-gleam beneath
                               the dark hat of the giver,

Who, as I came up the walk in summer moonlight
    and set foot to the porch step, rose with a cough from beside the hydrangea,
    and thrust the thing out at me, as though it were common for any total stranger
    to squat by one's door with a letter at night,
    at which, in surprise, I had stopped to stare (the address even then but a smudge)
    until at the burst of his laugh, like a mirthful catarrh,
    I turned, but before I could budge
    saw the pattering *V*'s of his shoe tips mar
    the moon-snowy dew of the yard,
    and be gone—an immigrant type of pointed toe and sleazy insouciance
                               more natural by far
    to some Mediterranean alley or merd-spangled *banlieue* than to any boulevard,

*

96

Or surely to Dadston, Tenn., and so I was stuck,
    for though my first thought was to drop the thing in the mail and forget the affair,
    on second glance I saw what at first I had missed, as though the words
                                  hadn't been there:
By Hand Only, and I was dumb-cluck
    enough to drive over to Nashville next day to find the address, but found
    you had blown, the rent in arrears, your bathroom a sty,
    and thus the metaphysical runaround
    which my life became, and for which I
    have mortgaged all, began,
    and I have found milk rotting in bottles inside the back door,
                              and newspapers knee-high
    the carrier had left and never got paid for, and once at my question
                                a child up and ran

Screaming like bloody murder to fall out of breath,
    and once in Dubuque you had sold real estate, and left with a church letter,
    Episcopal, High, and at the delicious New England farmhouse
                             your Llewellin setter
    was found in the woodshed, starved to death,
    and in Via Margutta you made the attempt, but someone smelled gas at the door
    in the nick of time, and you fooled with the female Fulbrights
    at the Deux Magots and the Flore,
    until the police caught you dead to rights—
    oh, it's all so human and sad,
    for money and love are terrible things with which to fill
                         all our human days and nights,
    and nobody blames you much, not even I, despite all the trouble I've had,
*

And still have, on your account, and if it were not
　　for encroaching age, new illness, and recurring effects of the beating
　　I took from those hoods in the bar in Frisco for the mere fact of merely repeating
　　that financial gossip, and from which I got
　　this bum gam, my defect in memory, and a slight stutter—
　　but as I was saying, were it not for my infirm years,
　　I would try to deliver the letter,
　　especially since I was moved nigh to tears
　　myself by the tale you'd been caught
　　crouching in the dark in the canna bed that pretties the lawn
　　　　　　　　　　　　　　　　of the orphanage where it appears
　　you were raised—yes, crooning among the ruined lilies to a teddy bear,
　　　　　　　　　　　　　　　not what a grown man ought

To be doing past midnight—but be that as it may,
　　there's little choice for my future course, given present circumstances,
　　and my conscience is clear, for I assure you I've not made a penny,
　　　　　　　　　　　　　　　　at least not expenses,
　　and so, on the basis of peasant hearsay
　　at the goatherd's below timber line, I will go up, and beyond the north face,
　　find that shelf where a last glacial kettle, beck, or cirque glints
　　blue steel to steel sky in that moon-place,
　　and there, while hands bleed and breath stints,
　　will, on a flat boulder not
　　far from the spot where you at night drink, leave the letter,
　　　　　　　　　　　　　　　and my obligation to all intents,
　　weighted by stones like a cairn, with a red bandanna to catch your eye, but what
＊

Good any word of money or love or more casual
    comfort may do now, God only knows, for one who by dog and gun
    has been hunted to the upper altitudes, for the time comes when all men will shun
    you, and you, like an animal,
    will crouch among the black boulders and whine under knife-edge of night-blast,
    waiting for hunger to drive you down to forage
    for bark, berries, mast,
    roots, rodents, grubs, and such garbage,
    or a sheep like the one you with teeth killed,
    for you are said to be capable now of all bestiality, and only your age
    makes you less dangerous; so, though I've never seen your face and have fulfilled

The trust, discretion, as well as perhaps a strange shame,
    overcomes curiosity, and from that high rubble of the world's wrack,
    will send me down to the darkness of trees until, having lost all track,
    I stand, bewildered, breath-bated and lame,
    at the edge of a clearing, to hear, as first birds stir, life lift now night's hasp,
    then see, in first dawn's drench and drama, the snow peak go gory,
    and the eagle will unlatch crag-clasp,
    fall, and at breaking of wing-furl, bark glory,
    and by that new light I shall seek
    the way, and my peace with God, and if in some taproom travelers pry
                                     into this story,
    I shall not reduce it to drunken marvel, assuming I know the tongue they speak.

I I I Man in the Street

Raise the stone, and there thou shalt find Me,
cleave the wood, there am I.

—THE SAYINGS OF JESUS

"Why are your eyes as big as saucers—big as saucers?"
I said to the man in the gray flannel suit.
And he said: "I see facts I can't refute—
Winners and losers,
Pickers and choosers,
Takers, refusers,
Users, abusers,
And my poor head, it spins like a top.
It spins and spins, and will not stop."
Thus said the young man I happened to meet,
Wearing his nice new Ivy League flannel suit down the sunlit street.

"What makes you shake like wind in the willows—wind in the willows?"
I said to the man in the black knit tie.
And he said: "I see things before my eye—
Jolly good fellows,
Glad-handers of hellos,
Fat windbags and bellows,
Plumpers of pillows,
And God's sweet air is like dust on my tongue,
And a man can't stand such things very long."
Thus said the young man I happened to meet,
Wearing his gray flannel suit and black knit tie down the sunlit street.

❋

"What makes your face flour-white as a miller's—white as a miller's?"
I said to the man in the Brooks Brothers shirt.
And he said: "I see things that can't help but hurt—
Backers and fillers,
Pickers and stealers,
Healers and killers,
Ticklers and feelers,
And I go to prepare a place for you,
For this location will never do."
Thus said the young man I happened to meet,
Wearing gray flannel suit, knit tie, and Brooks Brothers shirt down the sunlit street.

I V Switzerland

. . . *world-mecca for seekers of pleasure and health* . . .
—TRAVEL AGENCY BROCHURE

After lunch take the half-destroyed bodies and put them to bed.
For a time a mind's active behind the green gloom of the jalousie,
But soon each retires inside the appropriate head
To fondle, like childhood's stuffed bear, some favorite fallacy.

In their pairings the young, of course, have long since withdrawn,
But they take more time to come to the point of siesta:
There's the beach-fatigue and the first digestion to wait on,
So it's three by the time one's adjusted one's darling, and pressed her.

Here are many old friends you have known from long, long back,
Though of course under different names and with different faces.
Yes, they are the kind of whom you never lose track,
And there's little difference, one finds, between different places.

That's why travel is broadening—you can, for example, expect
The aging alcoholic you once knew in San Diego.
Or the lady theologian who in bed likes best her own intellect:
Lady Hulda House, *Cantab.*—for therapy now trying a dago.

There's the sweet young divorcée whose teacher once said she should write.
There's the athlete who stares at himself in the glass, by the hour.
There's the old man who can't forgive, and wakes in the night:
Forgive—forgive what? To remember is beyond his power.

✳

And the others and all, they all here re-enact
The acts you'd so shrewdly remarked at the very start,
When in other resorts you first met them—many, in fact,
In that high, highly advertised Switzerland of your own heart.

O God of the *steinbock's* great sun-leap—Thou spike in ice-chasm—
Let down Thy strong hand to all whom their fevers destroy
And past all their pain, need, greed, lip-biting, and spasm,
Deliver them all, young and old, to Thy health, named joy.

V   A Real Question Calling for Solution

Don't bother a bit, you are only a dream you are having,
And if when you wake your symptoms are not relieved,
That is only because you harbor a morbid craving
For belief in the old delusion in which you have always believed.

Yes, there was the year when every morning you ran
A mile before breakfast—yes, and the year you read
Virgil two hours just after lunch and began
Your practice of moral assessment, before the toothbrush and bed.

But love boiled down like porridge in a pot,
And beyond the far snow-fields westward, redder than hate,
The sun burned; and one night much better forgot,
Pity, like sputum, gleamed on the station floor-tiles, train late.

When you slept on a board you found your back much better.
When you took the mud baths you found that verse came easy.
When you slept with another woman you found that the letter
You owed your wife was a pleasure to write, gay now and teasy.

There once was a time when you thought you would understand
Many things, many things, including yourself, and learn Greek,
But light changes old landscape, and your own hand
Makes signs unseen in the dark, and lips move but do not speak,
*

For given that vulture and vector which is the stroke
Of the clock, absolute, on the bias of midnight, memory
Is nothing, is nothing, not even the memory of smoke
Dispersed on windless ease in the great fuddled head of the sky,

And all recollections are false, and all you suffer
Is only the punishment thought appropriate for guilt
You cuddle and kiss, and wish you had the crime for,
For the bitterest tears are those shed for milk—or blood—not spilt.

There is only one way, then, to make things hang together,
Which is to accept the logic of dream, and avoid
Night air, politics, French sauces, autumn weather,
And the thought that, on your awaking, identity may be destroyed.

VI Arrogant Law

Have you crouched with rifle, in woods, in autumn,
In earshot of water where at dawn deer come,
Through gold leafage drifting, through dawn-mist like mist,
And the blue steel sweats cold in your fist?
Have you stood on the gunwale and eyed blaze of sky,
Then with blaze blazing black in your inner eye,
Plunged—plunged to break the anchor's deep hold
On rock, where undercurrents thrill cold?
  Time unwinds like a falling spool.

Have you lain by your love, at night, by willows,
And heard the stream stumble, moon-drunk, at its shallows,
And heard the cows stir, sigh, and shift space,
Then seen how moonlight lay on the girl's face,
With her eyes hieratically closed, and your heart bulged
With what abrupt Truth to be divulged—
But desolate, desolate, turned from your love,
Knowing you'd never know what she then thought of?
  Time unwinds like a falling spool.

Have you stood beside your father's bed
While life retired from the knowledgeable head
To hole in some colding last lurking-place,
And standing there studied that strange face,
Which had endured thunder and even the tears
Of mercy in its human years,
But now, past such accident, seemed to withdraw
Into more arrogant dispensation, and law?
  Time unwinds like a falling spool.

TWO PIECES AFTER SUETONIUS

I   Apology for Domitian

He was not bad, as emperors go, not really—
Not like Tiberius cruel, or poor Nero silly.
The trouble was only that omens said he would die,
So what could he, mortal, do? Not worse, however, than you might, or I.

Suppose from long back you had known the very hour—
"Fear the fifth hour"—and yet for all your power
Couldn't strike it out from the day, or the day from the year,
Then wouldn't you have to strike something at least? If you did,
                                        would it seem so queer?

Suppose you were proud of your beauty, but baldness set in?
Suppose your good leg were dwindling to spindly and thin?
Wouldn't you, like Domitian, try the classic bed-stunt
To prove immortality on what was propped to bear the imperial brunt?

Suppose you had dreamed a gold hump sprouted out of your back,
And such a prosperous burden oppressed you to breath-lack;
Suppose lightning scorched the sheets in your own bedroom;
And from your own statue a storm yanked the name plate and chucked it
                                        into a tomb—

Well, it happened to him. Therefore, there's little surprise
That for hours he'd lock himself up to pull wings from flies.
Fly or man, what odds? He would wander his hall of moonstone,
Mirror-bright so he needn't look over his shoulder to see if he was alone.
*

107

Let's stop horsing around—it's not Domitian, it's you
We mean, and the omens are bad, very bad, and it's true
That virtue comes hard in face of the assiduous clock,
And music, at sunset, faint as a dream, is heard from beyond the burdock,

And as for Domitian, the first wound finds the groin,
And he claws like a cat, but the blade continues to go in,
And the body is huddled forth meanly, and what ritual
It gets is at night, and from his old nurse, a woman poor, nonpolitical.

I I Tiberius on Capri

1

All is nothing, nothing all:
To tired Tiberius soft sang the sea thus,
Under his cliff-palace wall.
The sea, in soft approach and repulse,
Sings thus, and Tiberius,
Sea-sad, stares past the dusking sea-pulse
Yonder, where come,
One now by one, the lights, far off, of Surrentum.
He stares in the blue dusk-fall,
For all is nothing, nothing all.

Let darkness up from Asia tower.
On that darkening island behind him *spintriae* now stir.
In grot and scented bower,
They titter, yawn, paint lip, grease thigh,
And debate what role each would prefer
When they project for the Emperor's eye
Their expertise
Of his Eastern lusts and complex Egyptian fantasies.
But darkward he stares in that hour,
Blank now in totality of power.

2

There once, on that goat island, I,
As dark fell, stood and stared where Europe stank.
Many were soon to die—
From acedia snatched, from depravity, virtue,
Or frolic, not knowing the reason, in rank
On rank hurled, or in bed, or in church, or
Dishing up supper,
Or in a dark doorway, loosening the girl's elastic to tup her,
While high in the night sky,
The murderous tear dropped from God's eye;

And faintly forefeeling, forefearing, all
That to fulfill our time, and heart, would come,
I stood on the crumbling wall
Of that foul place, and my lungs drew in
Scent of dry gorse on the night air of autumn,
And I seized, in dark, a small stone from that ruin,
And I made outcry
At the paradox of powers that would grind us like grain, small and dry.
Dark down, the stone, in its fall,
Found the sea: I could do that much, after all.

MORTMAIN

I   After Night Flight Son Reaches Bedside of Already Unconscious
Father, Whose Right Hand Lifts in a Spasmodic Gesture, as
Though Trying to Make Contact: 1955

In Time's concatenation and
Carnal conventicle, I,
Arriving, being flung through dark and
The abstract flight-grid of sky,
Saw rising from the sweated sheet and
Ruck of bedclothes ritualistically
Reordered by the paid hand
Of mercy—saw rising the hand—

Christ, start again! What was it I,
Standing there, travel-shaken, saw
Rising? What could it be that I,
Caught sudden in gut- or conscience-gnaw,
Saw rising out of the past, which I
Saw now as twisted bedclothes? Like law,
The hand rose cold from History
To claw at a star in the black sky,

But could not reach that far—oh, cannot!
And the star horribly burned, burns,
For in darkness the wax-white clutch could not
Reach it, and white hand on wrist-stem turns,
Lifts in last tension of tendon, but cannot
Make contact—*oh, oop-si-daisy,* churns
The sad heart, *oh, atta-boy, daddio's got*
One more shot in the locker, peas-porridge hot—
✳

III

But no. Like an eyelid the hand sank, strove
Downward, and in that darkening roar,
All things—all joy and the hope that strove,
The failed exam, the admired endeavor,
Prizes and prinkings, and the truth that strove,
And back of the Capitol, boyhood's first whore—
Were snatched from me, and I could not move,
Naked in that black blast of his love.

I I   A Dead Language: Circa 1885

Father dead, land lost, stepmother haggard with kids,
Big Brother skedaddling off to Mexico
To make his fortune, gold or cattle or cards,
What could he do but what we see him doing?
Cutting crossties for the first railroad in the region,
Sixteen and strong as a man—was a man, by God!—
And the double-bit bit into red oak, and in that rhythm,
In his head, all day, marched the Greek paradigm:
That was all that was his, and all he could carry all day with him.

Λέγω, λέγεις, λέγει, and the axe swung.
That was that year, and the next year we see him
Revolve in his dream between the piece goods and cheese,
In a crossroads store, between peppermint candy and plow-points,
While the eaves drip, and beyond the black trees of winter
Last light grays out, and in the ruts of the lane
Water gleams, sober as steel. That was that land,
And that was the life, and he reached out and
Took the dime from the gray-scaled palm of the Negro plowhand's hand.

'Εν ἀρχῇ ἦν ὁ λόγος: in the beginning
Was the word, but in the end was
What? At the mirror, lather on chin, with a razor
Big as a corn-knife, or so to the boy it seemed,
He stood, and said: 'Εν ἀρχῇ ἦν ὁ λόγος:
And laughed. And said: "That's Greek, now you know how it sounds!"
And laughed, and waved the bright blade like a toy.
And laughing from the deep of a dark conquest and joy,
Said: "Greek—but it wasn't for me. Let's get to breakfast, boy."

113

I I I Fox-Fire: 1956

Years later, I find the old grammar, yellowed. Night
Is falling. Ash flakes from the log. The log
Glows, winks, wanes. Westward, the sky,
In one small area redeemed from gray, bleeds dully.
Beyond my window, athwart that red west,
The spruce bough, though snow-burdened, looks black,
Not white. The world lives by the trick of the eye, the trick
Of the heart. I hold the book in my hand, but God
—In what mercy, if mercy?—will not let me weep. But I
Do not want to weep. I want to understand.

Oh, let me understand what is that sound,
Like wind, that fills the enormous dark of my head.
Beyond my head there is no wind, the room
Darkening, the world beyond the room darkening,
And no wind beyond to cleave, unclot, the thickening
Darkness. There must be a way to state the problem.
The statement of a problem, no doubt, determines solution.
If once, clear and distinct, I could state it, then God
Could no longer fall back on His old alibi of ignorance.
I hear now my small son laugh from a farther room.

*

I know he sits and laughs among his toys,
Teddy bear, letter blocks, yellow dump-truck, derrick, choo-choo—
Bright images, all, of Life's significance.
So I put the book on the shelf, beside my own grammar,
Unopened these thirty years, and leave the dark room,
And know that all night, while the constellations grind,
Beings with folded wings brood above that shelf,
Awe-struck and imbecile, and in the dark,
Amid History's vice and vacuity, that poor book burns
Like fox-fire in the black swamp of the world's error.

I V   In the Turpitude of Time: N. D.

In the turpitude of Time,
Hope dances on the razor edge.
I see those ever-healing feet
Tread the honed edge above despair.
I see the song-wet lip and tossing hair.

The leaf unfolds the autumn weather.
The heart spills the horizon's light.
In the woods, the hunter, weeping, kneels,
And the dappled fawn weeps in contrition
For its own beauty. I hear the toad's intercession

For us, and all, who do not know
How cause flows backward from effect
To bless the past occasion, and
How Time's tongue lifts only to tell,
Minute by minute, what truth the brave heart would fulfill.

Can we—oh, could we only—know
What annelid and osprey know,
And the stone, night-long, groans to divulge?
If only we could, then that star
That dawnward slants might sing to our human ear,

And joy, in daylight, run like feet,
And strength, in darkness, wait like hands,
And between the stone and the wind's voice
A silence wait to become our song:
In the heart's last kingdom only the old are young.

V   A Vision: Circa 1880

Out of the woods where pollen is a powder of gold
Shaken from pistil of oak minutely, and of maple,
And is falling, and the tulip tree lifts, not yet tarnished,
The last calyx, in whose chartreuse coolness recessed, dew,
Only this morning, lingered till noon—look,
Out of the woods, barefoot, the boy comes. He stands,
Hieratic, complete, in patched britches and that idleness of boyhood
Which asks nothing and is its own fulfilment:
In his hand a wand of peeled willow, boy-idle and aimless.

Poised between woods and the pasture, sun-green and green shadow,
Hair sweat-dark, brow bearing a smudge of gold pollen, lips
Parted in some near-smile of boyhood bemusement,
Dangling the willow, he stands, and I—I stare
Down the tube and darkening corridor of Time
That breaks, like tears, upon that sunlit space,
And staring, I know who he is, and would cry out.
Out of my knowledge, I would cry out and say:
Listen! Say: *Listen! I know—oh, I know—let me tell you!*

That scene is in Trigg County, and I see it.
Trigg County is in Kentucky, and I have been there,
But never remember the spring there. I remember
A land of cedar-shade, blue, and the purl of limewater,
But the pasture parched, and the voice of the lost joree
Unrelenting as conscience, and sick, and the afternoon throbs,
And the sun's hot eye on the dry leaf shrivels the aphid,
And the sun's heel does violence in the corn-balk.
That is what I remember, and so the scene

✻

I had seen just now in the mind's eye, vernal,
Is altered, and I strive to cry across the dry pasture,
But cannot, nor move, for my feet, like dry corn-roots, cleave
Into the hard earth, and my tongue makes only the dry,
Slight sound of wind on the autumn corn-blade. The boy,
With imperial calm, crosses a space, rejoins
The shadow of woods, but pauses, turns, grins once,
And is gone. And one high oak leaf stirs gray, and the air,
Stirring, freshens to the far favor of rain.

SOME QUIET, PLAIN POEMS

I Ornithology in a World of Flux

It was only a bird call at evening, unidentified,
As I came from the spring with water, across the rocky back-pasture;
But so still I stood sky above was not stiller than sky in pail-water.

Years pass, all places and faces fade, some people have died,
And I stand in a far land, the evening still, and am at last sure
That I miss more that stillness at bird-call than some things that were to fail later.

I I   Holly and Hickory

Rain, all night, taps the holly.
It ticks like a telegraph on the pane.
If awake in that house, meditating some old folly
Or trying to live an old pleasure again,
I could hear it sluicing the ruts in the lane.

Rain beats down the last leaf of hickory,
But where I lie now rain-sounds hint less
At benign sleight of the seasons, or Time's adept trickery,
And with years I feel less joy or distress
To hear water moving in wheel ruts, star-glintless,

And if any car comes now up that lane,
It carries nobody I could know,
And who wakes in that house now to hear the rain
May fall back to sleep—as I, long ago,
Who dreamed dawnward; and would rise to go.

III   The Well House

What happened there, it was not much,
But was enough. If you come back,
Not much may be *too much,* even if you have your old knack
Of stillness, and do not touch
A thing, a broken toy or rusted tool or any such
Object you happen to find
Hidden where, uncontrolled, grass and weeds bend.

The clematis that latches the door
Of the ruinous well house, you might break it.
Though guessing the water foul now, and not thirsting to take it,
With thirst from those years before
You might lean over the coping to stare at the water's dark-glinting floor.
Yes, that might be the event
To change *not much* to *too much,* and more than meant.

Yes, Truth is always in balance, and
Not much can become *too much* so quick.
Suppose you came back and found your heart suddenly sick,
And covered your sight with your hand:
Your tears might mean more than the thing you wept for but did not understand.
Yes, something might happen there
If you came back—even if you just stood to stare.

I V In Moonlight, Somewhere, They Are Singing

Under the maples at moonrise—
Moon whitening top leaf of the white oak
That rose from the dark mass of maples and range of eyes—
They were singing together, and I woke

From my sleep to the whiteness of moon-fire,
And deep from their dark maples, I
Could hear the two voices shake silver and free, and aspire
To be lost in moon-vastness of the sky.

My young aunt and her young husband
From their dark maples sang, and though
Too young to know what they meant I was happy and
So slept, for I knew I would come to know.

But what of the old man awake there,
As the voices, like vine, climbed up moonlight?
What thought did he think of past time as they twined bright in moon-air,
And veined, with their silver, the moon-flesh of night?

Far off, I recall, in the barn lot,
A mule stamped, once; but the song then
Was over, and for that night, or forever, would not
Resume—but should it again,

Now years later, wake me to white moon-fire
On pillow, high oak leaf, and far field,
I should hope to find imaged in whatever new voices aspire
Some life-faith yet, by my years, unrepealed.

V In Italian They Call the Bird *Civetta*

The evening drooped toward owl-call,
The small moon slid pale down the sky,
Dark was decisive in cedars,
But dust down the lane dreamed pale,
And my feet stirred that pale dust there—
Ah, I see that Kentucky scene
Now only behind my shut eyelids,
As in this far land I stand
At the selfsame ambiguous hour
In the heart's ambiguity,
And Time is crumpled like paper
Crushed in my hand, while here
  The thin moon slants pale down the pale sky,
  And the small owl mourns from the moat.

This small owl calls from the moat now,
And across all the years and miles that
Are the only Truth I have learned,
That other owl answers him;
So back from the present owl-call
Burns backward the blaze of Time,
And the passage of years, like a tire's scream,
Fades to nothing while the reply
Of a dew-damp and downy lost throat now
Quavers from that home-dark,
To frame, between owl-call and owl-call,
Life's bright parenthesis.
  The thin moon slants pale down the pale sky:
  The small owl mourns from the moat.

123

V I Debate: Question, Quarry, Dream

Asking what, asking what?—all a boy's afternoon,
Squatting in the canebrake where the muskrat will come.
Muskrat, muskrat, please now, please, come soon.
He comes, stares, goes, lets the question resume.
He has taken whatever answer may be down to his mud-burrow gloom.

Seeking what, seeking what?—foot soft in cedar-shade.
Was that a deer-flag white past windfall and fern?
No, but by bluffside lurk powers and in the fern-glade
Tall presences, standing all night, like white fox-fire burn.
The small fox lays his head in your hand now and weeps that you go, not to return.

Dreaming what, dreaming what?—lying on the hill at twilight,
The still air stirred only by moth wing, and the last stain of sun
Fading to moth-sky, blood-red to moth-white and starlight,
And Time leans down to kiss the heart's ambition,
While far away, before moonrise, come the town lights, one by one.

Long since that time I have walked night streets, heel-iron
Clicking the stone, and in dark in windows have stared.
Question, quarry, dream—I have vented my ire on
My own heart that, ignorant and untoward,
Yearns for an absolute that Time would, I thought, have prepared,

*

But has not yet. Well, let us debate
The issue. But under a tight roof, clutching a toy,
My son now sleeps, and when the hour grows late,
I shall go forth where the cold constellations deploy
And lift up my eyes to consider more strictly the appalling logic of joy.

BALLAD: BETWEEN THE BOXCARS (1923)

I   I Can't Even Remember the Name

I can't even remember the name of the one who fell
Flat on his ass, on the cinders, between the boxcars.
I can't even remember whether he got off his yell
Before what happened had happened between the boxcars.

But whether or not he managed to get off his yell,
I remember its shape on his mouth, between the boxcars,
And it was shape that yours would be too if you fell
Flat on your ass, on the cinders, between the boxcars.

And there's one sure thing you had better remember well,
You go for the grip at the front, not the back, of the boxcars.
Miss the front, you're knocked off—miss the back, you never can tell
But you're flat on your ass, on the cinders, between the boxcars.

He was fifteen and old enough to know perfectly well
You go for the grip at the front, not the back, of the boxcars,
But he was the kind of smart aleck you always can tell
Will end flat on his ass, on the cinders, between the boxcars.

Suppose I remembered his name, then what the hell
Good would it do him now between the boxcars?
But it might mean something to me if I could tell
You the name of the one who fell between the boxcars.

I I He Was Formidable

He was formidable, he was, the little booger,
As he spat in his hands and picked up the Louisville Slugger,
And at that bat-crack
Around those bases he could sure ball the jack,
And if from the outfield the peg had beat him home,
He would slide in slick, like a knife in a nigger.
So we dreamed of an afternoon to come,
In the Series, the ninth-inning hush, in the Yankee Stadium,
Sun low, score tied, bases full, two out, and he'd waltz to the plate with his grin—
But no, oh no, not now, not ever! for in
That umpireless rhubarb and steel-heeled hugger-mugger,
   He got spiked sliding home, got spiked between the boxcars.

Oh, his hair was brown-bright as a chestnut, sun-glinting and curly,
And that lip that smiled boy-sweet could go, of a sudden, man-surly,
And the way he was built
Made the girls in his grade in the dark stare, and finger the quilt.
Yes, he was the kind you know born to give many delight,
And entering on such life-labor early,
Would have moved, bemused, in that rhythm and rite,
Through blood-throbbing blackness and moon-gleam
                       and pearly thigh-glimmer of night,
To the exquisite glut: *Woman Slays Self for Love,* as the tabloids would tell—
But no, never now! Like a kid in his first brothel,
In that hot clasp and loveless hurly-burly,
   He spilled, as boys may, too soon, between the boxcars.

*

127

Oh, he might have managed the best supermarket in town,
Bright with banners and chrome, where housewives push carts up and down,
And morning and night
Walked the street with his credit *A*-rated and blood pressure right,
His boy a dentist in Nashville, his girl at State Normal;
Or a scientist flushed with *Time*-cover renown
For vaccine, or bomb, or smog removal;
Or a hero with phiz like hewn cedar, though young for the stars of a general,
Descending the steps of his personal plane to view the home-town unveiling.
But no, never now!—battle-cunning, the test tube, retailing,
All, all, in a helter-skeltering mishmash thrown
    To that clobber and grind, too soon, between the boxcars.

But what is success, or failure, at the last?
The newspaper whirled down the track when the through freight has passed
Will sink from that gust
To be of such value as it intrinsically must,
And why should we grieve for the name that boy might have made
To be printed on newsprint like that, for that blast
To whirl with the wheels' fanfaronade,
When we cannot even remember his name, nor humbly have prayed
That when that blunt grossness, slam-banging, bang-slamming, blots black
                                        the last blue flash of sky,
And our own lips utter the crazed organism's cry,
We may know the poor self not alone, but with all who are cast
    To that clobber, and clobber, and scream, between the boxcars?

TWO STUDIES IN IDEALISM: SHORT SURVEY OF AMERICAN, AND HUMAN, HISTORY

FOR ALLAN NEVINS

I   Bear Track Plantation: Shortly After Shiloh

Two things a man's built for, killing and you-know-what.
As for you-know-what, I reckon I taken my share,
Bed-ease or bush-whack, but killing—hell, three's all I got,
And he promised me ten, Jeff Davis, the bastard. 'Taint fair.

It ain't fair, a man rides and knows he won't live forever,
And a man needs something to take with him when he dies.
Ain't much worth taking, but what happens under the cover
Or at the steel-point—yeah, that look in their eyes.

That same look, it comes in their eyes when you give 'em the business.
It's something a man can hang on to, come black-frost or sun.
Come hell or high water, it's something to save from the mess,
No matter whatever else you never got done.

For a second it seems like a man can know what he lives for,
When those eyelids go waggle, or maybe the eyes pop wide,
And that look comes there. Yeah, Christ, then you know who you are—
And will maybe remember that much even after you've died.

But now I lie worrying what look my own eyes got
When that Blue-Belly caught me off balance. Did my look mean then
That I'd honed for something not killing or you-know-what?
Hell, no. I'd lie easy if Jeff had just give me that ten.

II   Harvard '61: Battle Fatigue

I didn't mind dying—it wasn't that at all.
It behooves a man to prove manhood by dying for Right.
If you die for Right that fact is your dearest requital,
But you find it disturbing when others die who simply haven't the right.

Why should they die with that obscene insouciance?
They seem to insult the principle of your own death.
Touch pitch, be defiled: it was hard to keep proper distance
From such unprincipled wastrels of blood and profligates of breath.

I tried to slay without rancor, and often succeeded.
I tried to keep the heart pure, though my hand took stain.
But they made it so hard for me, the way they proceeded
To parody with their own dying that Death which only Right should sustain.

Time passed. It got worse. It seemed like a plot against me.
I said they had made their own evil bed and lay on it,
But they grinned in the dark—they grinned—and I yet see
That last one. At woods-edge we held, and over the stubble they came with bayonet.

He uttered his yell, he was there!—teeth yellow, some missing.
Why, he's old as my father, I thought, finger frozen on trigger.
I saw the ambeer on his whiskers, heard the old breath hissing.
The puncture came small on his chest. 'Twas nothing. The stain then got bigger.

*

And he said: "Why, son, you done done it—I figgered I'd skeered ye."
Said: "Son, you look puke-pale. Buck up! If it hadn't been you,
Some other young squirt would a-done it." I stood, and weirdly
The tumult of battle went soundless, like gesture in dream. And I was dead, too.

Dead, and had died for the Right, as I had a right to,
And glad to be dead, and hold my residence
Beyond life's awful illogic, and the world's stew,
Where people who haven't the right just die, with ghastly impertinence.

Autumnal Equinox on Mediterranean Beach

Sail-bellyer, exciter of boys, come bang
To smithereens doors, and see if I give a hang,

For I am sick of summer and the insane glitter
Of sea sun-bit, and the wavelets that bicker and titter,

And the fat girls that hang out brown breasts like fruit overripe,
And the thin ones flung pale in rock-shadow, goose-pimpled as tripe,

And the young men who pose on the headlands like ads for Jantzen,
And the old who would do so much better to keep proper pants on,

And all Latin faeces one finds, like jewels, in the sand,
And the gaze of the small, sweet octopus fondling your hand.

Come howl like a prophet the season's righteous anger,
And knock down our idols with crash, bang, or clangor.

Blow the cat's fur furry sideways, make dogs bark,
Blow the hen's tail feathers forward past the pink mark,

Snatch the laundry off the line, like youth away,
Blow plastered hair off the bald spot, lift toupee.

Come blow old women's skirts, bring Truth to light,
Though at such age morn's all the same as night.
✲

Come swirl old picnic papers to very sky-height,
And make gulls gabble in fury at such breach of their air-right.

Kick up the bay now, make a mess of it,
Fling spume in our sinful faces, like God's spit,

For now all our pleasures, like peaches, get rotten, not riper,
And summer is over, and time to pay the piper,

And be glad to do it, for man's not made for much pleasure—
Certainly not for joy, unless it's cut down to his measure.

Yes, kick the garbage pail, and scatter garbage,
That the cat flee forth with a fish-head, the housewife rage,

For pain and pleasure balance in God's year—
Though *whose* is *which* is not your problem here,

And perhaps not even God's. So bang, wind, batter,
While human hearts do the bookkeeping in this matter.

I   Knockety-Knockety-Knock

Hickory-dickory-dock—
The mouse ran up the clock.
The clock struck one,
And I fell down,
Hickory-dickory-dock.
God let me fall down,
And I tore my nightgown,
And knockety-knockety-knock,
As I lie on the floor,
Someone's at the door—
Hickory-dickory-dock.

Hickory-dickory-dock—
The mouse runs up the clock.
My father took me
For a ride on his knee,
Hickory-dickory-dock.
But then things were nice,
With no awful mice,
And no knockety-knockety-knock,
And my head didn't spin
When the strange foot came in—
Hickory-dickory-dock.

*

Hickory-dickory-dock—
The mouse runs up the clock.
When I'd wake in the night,
Mother held me tight,
Hickory-dickory-dock.
Then dreams were just dreams,
And not, as it now seems,
A knockety-knockety-knock
That walks in at the door
As I lie on the floor—
Hickory-dickory-dock.

Hickory-dickory-dock—
The mouse ran up the clock,
And the clock struck one
And my poor head spun,
Hickory-dickory-dock,
And Ma's deader than mackerel,
And Pa pickled as pickerel,
And oh! knockety-knockety-knock,
God's red eyes glare
From sockets of dark air—
Knockety-knockety-knock.

I I News of Unexpected Demise of Little Boy Blue

Little Boy Blue, come blow your horn,
The sheep's in the meadow, the cow's in the corn.
Little Boy, will you make me stand and call
From first dawn-robin to last dew-fall?
It's no excuse you are young and careless,
With your thing-a-bob little and your little chest hairless,
For people have duties to perform at all ages—
Hurry up, Little Boy, or I'll dock your wages.

Come blow your horn, Little Boy Blue,
Or I'll make your bottom the bluest part of you.
Come blow your horn, you Little Gold-bricker,
Or I'll snatch you baldheaded in a wink, or quicker.
Little Boy, you'll get no more ice cream.
Nobody will come when you have a bad dream.
Where is that pretty little horn I gave you?
I simply won't tolerate such behavior.

I should have known you'd be derelict.
From a family like yours what can we expect?
Got by man just for the frig,
Born of woman, and she grunted like a pig,
Dropped in the world like a package of offal,
Demanding love with wail and snuffle,
Lost in the world and the trees were tall—
You Little Wretch, don't you hear me call!

❋

A plague and a pox on such a bad boy.
I know you are hiding just to annoy.
You reflect no credit on the human race.
You stand in need of prayer and grace.
Where's that Little Wretch that tends the sheep?

He's under the haystack, fast asleep.

Well, damn it, go wake him!

                    No, not I—
I can only walk the green fields, and cry.

I I I Mother Makes the Biscuits

Mother makes the biscuits,
Father makes the laws,
Grandma wets the bed sometimes,
Kitty-cats have claws.

Mother sweeps the kitchen,
Father milks the cow,
Grandpa leaves his pants unbuttoned,
Puppy-dogs bark, *bow-wow*.

All do as God intends,
The sun sets in the west,
Father shaves his chin, *scrape-scrape,*
Mother knows best.

Clap hands, children,
Clap hands and sing!
Hold hands together, children,
And dance in a ring,

For the green worm sings on the leaf,
The black beetle folds hands to pray,
And the stones in the field wash their faces clean
To meet break of day.

*

But we may see this only
Because all night we have stared
At the black miles past where stars are
Till the stars disappeared.

I Nightmare of Mouse

It was there, but I said it couldn't be true in daylight.
It was there, but I said it was only a trick of starlight.
It was there, but I said to believe it would take a fool,
And I wasn't, so didn't—till teeth crunched on my skull.

I I Colloquy with Cockroach

I know I smell. But everyone does, somewhat.
I smell this way only because I crawl down the drain.
I've no slightest idea how you got the smell you've got.
No, I haven't time now—it might take you too long to explain.

I I I   Cricket, on Kitchen Floor, Enters History

History, shaped like white hen,
Walked in at kitchen door.
Beak clicked once on stone floor.
Out door walked hen then;
But will, no doubt, come again.

I V   Grasshopper Tries to Break Solipsism

Sing *summer, summer,* sing *summer* summerlong—
For God is light, oh, I love Him, love is my song.
I sing, for I must, for God, if I didn't, would weep,
And over all things, all night, His despair, like ice, creep.

From **PROMISES**

Poems   1954–1956

TO A LITTLE GIRL, ONE YEAR OLD, IN A RUINED FORTRESS

TO ROSANNA

I Sirocco

To a place of ruined stone we brought you, and sea-reaches.
Rocca: fortress, hawk-heel, lion-paw, clamped on a hill.
A hill, no. On a sea cliff, and crag-cocked, the embrasures commanding the beaches,
Range easy, with most fastidious mathematic and skill.

Philipus me fecit: he of Spain, the black-browed, the anguished,
For whom nothing prospered, though he loved God.
His arms, a great scutcheon of stone, once over the drawbridge, have languished
Now long in the moat, under garbage; at moat-brink, rosemary with blue,
                       thistle with gold bloom, nod.

Sun blaze and cloud tatter, now the sirocco, the dust swirl is swirled
Over the bay face, mounts air like gold gauze whirled; it traverses
                       the blaze-blue of water.
We have brought you where geometry of a military rigor survives
                       its own ruined world,
And sun regilds your gilt hair, in the midst of your laughter.

Rosemary, thistle, clutch stone. Far hangs Giannutri in blue air. Far to that
                       blueness the heart aches,
And on the exposed approaches the last gold of gorse bloom, in the sirocco, shakes.

I I Gull's Cry

White goose by palm tree, palm ragged, among stones the white oleander,
And the she-goat, brown, under pink oleanders, waits.
I do not think that anything in the world will move, not goat, not gander.
Goat droppings are fresh in the hot dust; not yet the beetle; the sun beats,

And under blue shade of the mountain, over blue-braiding sea-shadow,
The gull hangs white; whiter than white against the mountain-mass,
The gull extends motionless on a shelf of air, on the substance of shadow.
The gull, at an eye-blink, will, into the astonishing statement of sun, pass.

All night, next door, the defective child cried; now squats in the dust
                                        where the lizard goes.
The wife of the *gobbo* sits under vine leaves, she suffers, her eyes glare.
The engaged ones sit in the privacy of bemusement, heads bent: the classic pose.
Let the beetle work, the gull comment the irrelevant anguish of air,

But at your laughter let the molecular dance of the stone-dark
                                        glimmer like joy in the stone's dream,
And in that moment of possibility, let *gobbo, gobbo's* wife, and us, and all,
                                        take hands and sing: *redeem, redeem!*

I I I   The Child Next Door

The child next door is defective because the mother,
Seven brats already in that purlieu of dirt,
Took a pill, or did something to herself she thought would not hurt,
But it did, and no good, for there came this monstrous other.

The sister is twelve. Is beautiful like a saint.
Sits with the monster all day, with pure love, calm eyes.
Has taught it a trick, to make *ciao,* Italian-wise.
It crooks hand in that greeting. She smiles her smile without taint.

I come, and her triptych beauty and joy stir hate
—Is it hate?—in my heart. Fool, doesn't she know that the process
Is not that joyous or simple, to bless, or unbless,
The malfeasance of nature or the filth of fate?

Can it bind or loose, that beauty in that kind,
Beauty of benediction? We must trust our hope to prevail
That heart-joy in beauty be wisdom, before beauty fail
And be gathered like air in the ruck of the world's wind!

I think of your goldness, of joy, but how empires grind, stars are hurled.
I smile stiff, saying *ciao,* saying *ciao,* and think: *This is the world.*

I V   The Flower

Above the beach, the vineyard
Terrace breaks to the seaward
Drop, where the cliffs fail
To a clutter of manganese shale.
Some is purple, some powdery-pale.
But the black lava-chunks stand off
The sea's grind, or indolent chuff.
The lava will withstand
The sea's beat, or insinuant hand,
And protect our patch of sand.

It is late. The path from the beach
Crawls up. I take you. We reach
The vineyard, and at that path angle
The hedge obtrudes a tangle
Of leaf and green bulge and a wrangle
Bee-drowsy and blowsy with white bloom,
Scarcely giving the passer-by room.
We know that the blossomy mass
Will brush our heads as we pass,
And at knee there's gold gorse and blue clover,
And at ankle, blue *malva* all over—
Plus plants I don't recognize
With my non-botanical eyes.
We approach, but before we get there,
If no breeze stirs that green lair,
The scent and sun-honey of air
Is too sweet comfortably to bear.

*

I carry you up the hill.
In my arms you are still.
We approach your special place,
And I am watching your face
To see the sweet puzzlement grow,
And then recognition glow.
Recognition explodes in delight.
You leap like spray, or like light.
Despite my arm's tightness,
You leap in gold-glitter and brightness.
You leap like a fish-flash in bright air,
And reach out. Yes, I'm well aware
That this is the spot, and hour,
For you to demand your flower.

When first we came this way
Up from the beach, that day
That seems now so long ago,
We moved bemused and slow
In the season's pulse and flow.
Bemused with sea, and slow
With June heat and perfume,
We paused here, and plucked you a bloom.
So here you always demand
Your flower to hold in your hand,
And the flower must be white,
For you have your own ways to compel
Observance of this ritual.
You hold it and sing with delight.
And your mother, for our own delight,
Picks one of the blue flowers there,
To put in your yellow hair.
That done, we go on our way
Up the hill, toward the end of the day.
*

But the season has thinned out.
From the bay edge below, the shout
Of a late bather reaches our ear,
Coming to the vineyard here
By more than distance thinned.
The bay is in shadow, the wind
Nags the shore to white.
The mountain prepares the night.

By the vineyard we have found
No bloom worthily white,
And the few we have found
Not disintegrated to the ground
Are by season and sea-salt browned.
We give the best one to you.
It is ruined, but will have to do.
Somewhat better the blue blossoms fare.
So we find one for your hair,
And you sing as though human need
Were not for perfection. We proceed
Past floss-borne or sloughed-off seed,
Past curled leaf and dry pod,
And the blue blossom will nod
With your head's drowsy gold nod.

Let all seasons pace their power,
As this has paced to this hour.
Let season and season devise
Their possibilities.
Let the future reassess

All past joy, and past distress,
Till we know Time's deep intent,
And the last integument
Of the past shall be rent
To show how all things bent
Their energies to that hour
When you first demanded your flower.

Yes, in that image let
Both past and future forget,
In clasped communal ease,
Their brute identities.

The path lifts up ahead
To the *rocca,* supper, bed.
We move in the mountain's shade.
The mountain is at our back.
But ahead, climbs the coast-cliff track.
The valley between is dim.
Ahead, on the cliff rim,
The *rocca* clasps its height.
It accepts the incipient night.

Just once we look back.
On sunset, a white gull is black.
It hangs over the mountain crest.
It hangs on that saffron west.
It makes its outcry.
It slides down the sky.

*

East now, it catches the light.
Its black has gone again white,
And over the *rocca's* height
It gleams in the last light.

Now it sinks from our sight.
Beyond the cliff is night.

It sank on unruffled wing.
We hear the sea rustling.

V   Colder Fire

It rained toward day. The morning came sad and white
With silver of sea-sadness and defection of season.
Our joys and convictions are sure, but in that wan light
We moved—your mother and I—in muteness of spirit past logical reason.

Now sun, afternoon, and again summer-glitter on sea.
As you to a bright toy, the heart leaps. The heart unlocks
Joy, though we know, shamefaced, the heart's weather should not be
Merely a reflex to a solstice, or sport of some aggrieved equinox.

No, the heart should be steadfast: I know that.
And I sit in the late-sunny lee of the watch-house,
At the fortress point, you on my knee now, and the late
White butterflies over gold thistle conduct their ritual carouse.

In whisperless carnival, in vehemence of gossamer,
Pale ghosts of pale passions of air, the white wings weave.
In tingle and tangle of arabesque, they mount light, pair by pair,
As though that tall light were eternal indeed, not merely the summer's reprieve.

You leap on my knee, you exclaim at the sun-stung gyration.
And the upper air stirs, as though the vast stillness of sky
Had stirred in its sunlit sleep and made a suspiration,
A luxurious languor of breath, as after love, there is a sigh.

*

But enough, for the highest sun-scintillant pair are gone
Seaward, past rampart and cliff borne, over blue sea-gleam.
Close to my chair, to a thistle, a butterfly sinks now, flight done.
By the gold bloom of thistle, white wings pulse under the sky's dream.

The sky's dream is enormous, I lift up my eyes.
In sunlight a tatter of mist clings high on the mountain-mass.
The mountain is under the sky, and there the gray scarps rise
Past paths where on their appointed occasions men climb, and pass.

Past grain-patch, last apron of vineyard, last terrace of olive,
Past chestnut, past cork grove, where the last carts can go,
Past camp of the charcoal maker, where coals glow in the black hive,
The scarps, gray, rise up. Above them is that place I know.

The pines are there, they are large, in a deep recess—
Shelf above scarp, enclave of rock, a glade
Benched and withdrawn in the mountain-mass, under the peak's duress.
We came there—your mother and I—and rested in that severe shade.

Pine-blackness mist-tangled, the peak black above: the glade gives
On the empty threshold of air, the hawk-hung delight
Of distance unspooled and bright space spilled—ah, the heart thrives!
We stood in that shade and saw sea and land lift in the far light.

Now the butterflies dance, time-tattered and disarrayed.
I watch them. I think how above that far scarp's sunlit wall
Mist threads in silence the darkness of boughs, and in that shade
Condensed moisture gathers at a needle-tip. It glitters, will fall.

*

I cannot interpret for you this collocation
Of memories. You will live your own life, and contrive
The language of your own heart, but let that conversation,
In the last analysis, be always of whatever truth you would live.

For fire flames but in the heart of a colder fire.
All voice is but echo caught from a soundless voice.
Height is not deprivation of valley, nor defect of desire,
But defines, for the fortunate, that joy in which all joys should rejoice.

PROMISES

TO GABRIEL

I What Was the Promise That Smiled from the Maples
at Evening?

What was the promise that smiled from the maples at evening?
Smiling dim from the shadow, recessed? What language of leaf-lip?
And the heels of the fathers click on the concrete, returning,
Each aware of his own unspecified burden, at sun-dip.
In first darkness hydrangeas float white in their spectral precinct.
Beneath pale hydrangeas the first firefly utters cold burning.
The sun is well down, the first star has now winked.

What was the promise when bullbats dizzied the sunset?
They skimmer and skitter in gold light at great height.
The guns of big boys on the common go *boom,* past regret.
Boys shout when the bullbat spins down in that gold light.
"Too little to shoot"—but next year you'll be a big boy.
So shout now and pick up the bird—why, that's blood, it is wet.
Its eyes are still open, your heart in the throat swells like joy.

What was the promise when, after the last light had died,
Children gravely, down walks, in spring dark, under maples, drew
Trains of shoe boxes, empty, with windows, with candles inside,
Going *chuck-chuck,* and blowing for crossings, lonely, *oo-oo?*
But on impulse you fled, and they called, called across the dark lawn,
Long calling your name, who now lay in the darkness to hide,
While the sad little trains glimmer on under maples, and on.

*

What was the promise when, after the dying was done,
All the long years before, like burnt paper, flared into black,
And the house shrunk to silence, the odor of flowers near gone?
Recollection of childhood was natural: cold gust at the back.
What door on the dark flings open, then suddenly bangs?
Yes, something was lost in between, but it's long, the way back.
You sleep, but in sleep hear a door that creaks where it hangs.

Long since, in a cold and coagulate evening, I've stood
Where they slept, the long dead, and the farms and far woods fled away,
And a gray light prevailed and both landscape and heart were subdued.
Then sudden, the ground at my feet was like glass, and I say
What I saw, saw deep down—with their fleshly habiliments rent
But their bones in a phosphorus of glory agleam, there they lay,
Side by side, Ruth and Robert. But quickly that light was spent.

Earth was earth, and in earth-dark the glow died, therefore I lifted
My gaze to that world which had once been the heart's familiar,
Swell of woods and far field-sweep, in dusk by stream-gleams now wefted,
Railroad yonder and coal chute, town roofs far under the first star.
Then her voice, long forgotten, calm in silence, said: "Child."
And his, with the calm of a night field, or far star:
"We died only that every promise might be fulfilled."

159

I I   Court-Martial

Under the cedar tree,
He would sit, all summer, with me:
An old man and small grandson
Withdrawn from the heat of the sun.

Captain, cavalry, C.S.A.,
An old man, now shrunken, gray,
Pointed beard clipped the classic way,
Tendons long gone crank and wry,
And long shrunken the cavalryman's thigh
Under the pale-washed blue jean.
His pipe smoke lifts, serene
Beneath boughs of the evergreen,
With sunlight dappling between.
I see him now, as once seen.

Light throbs the far hill.
The boughs of the cedar are still.

His years like landscape lie
Spread to the backward eye
In life's long irony.
All the old hoofbeats fade
In the calm of the cedar shade,
Where only the murmur and hum
Of the far farm, and summer, now come.
He can forget all—forget
Even mortgage and lien and debt,

Cutworm and hail and drouth,
Bang's disease, hoof-and-mouth,
Barn sagging and broken house.
Now in the shade, adrowse,
At last he can sit, or rouse
To light a pipe, or say to me
Some scrap of old poetry—
Byron or Burns—and idly
The words glimmer and fade
Like sparks in the dark of his head.

In the dust by his chair
I undertook to repair
The mistakes of his old war.
Hunched on that toy terrain,
Campaign by campaign,
I sought, somehow, to untie
The knot of History,
For in our shade I knew
That only the Truth is true,
That life is only the act
To transfigure all fact,
And life is only a story
And death is only the glory
Of the telling of the story,
And the *done* and the *to-be-done*
In that timelessness were one,
Beyond the poor *being done*.

The afternoon stood still.
Sun dazzled the far hill.
✳

It was only a chance word
That a chance recollection had stirred.
"Guerrilla—what's that?" I said.
"Bushwhackers, we called 'em," he said.
"Were they on the Yankee side?"
"Son, they didn't have any side.
Just out to plunder and ride
And hell-rake the pore countryside.
Just out for themselves, so, son,
If you happened to run across one,
Or better, laid hand to a passel,
No need to be squeamish, or wrestle
Too long with your conscience. But if—"
He paused, raised his pipe, took a whiff—
"If your stomach or conscience was queasy,
You could make it all regular, easy.

"By the road, find some shade, a nice patch.
Even hackberry does, at a scratch.
Find a spring with some cress fresh beside it,
Growing rank enough to nigh hide it.
Lord, a man can sure thirst when you ride.
Yes, find you a nice spot to bide.
Bide sweet when you can when you ride.
Order halt, let the heat-daze subside.
Put your pickets, vedettes out, dismount.
Water horses, grease gall, take count,
And while the men rest and jaw,
You and two lieutenants talk law.
Brevitatem justitia amat.
Time is short—hell, a rope is—that's that."
*

That was that, and the old eyes were closed.
On a knee one old hand reposed,
Fingers crooked on the cob pipe, where
The last smoke raveled blue up the air.
Every tale ravels out to an end.
But smoke rose, did not waver or bend.
It unspooled, wouldn't stop, wouldn't end.

"By God—" and he jerked up his head.
"By God, they deserved it," he said.
"Don't look at me that way," he said.
"By God—" and the old eyes glared red.
Then shut in the cedar shade.

The head slept in that dusk the boughs made.
The world's silence made me afraid.
Then a July-fly, somewhere,
Like silk ripping, ripped the bright air.
Then stopped. Sweat broke in my hair.

I snatched my gaze away.
I swung to the blazing day.
Ruined lawn, raw house swam in light.
The far woods swam in my sight.
Throbbing, the fields fell away
Under the blaze of day.

Calmly then, out of the sky,
Blotting the sun's blazing eye,
He rode. He was large in the sky.
Behind, shadow massed, slow, and grew
Like cloud on the sky's summer blue.
Out of that shade-mass he drew.

To the great saddle's sway, he swung,
Not old now, not old now—but young,
Great cavalry boots to the thigh,
No speculation in eye.
Then clotting behind him, and dim,
Clot by clot, from the shadow behind him,
They took shape, enormous in air.
Behind him, enormous, they hung there:

Ornaments of the old rope,
Each face outraged, agape,
Not yet believing it true—
The hairy jaw askew,
Tongue out, out-staring eye,
And the spittle not yet dry
That was uttered with the last cry.

The horseman does not look back.
Blank-eyed, he continues his track,
Riding toward me there,
Through the darkening air.

The world is real. It is there.

I I I   Gold Glade

Wandering, in autumn, the woods of boyhood,
Where cedars, black, thick, rode the ridge,
Heart aimless as rifle, in boy-blankness of mood,
I came where the ridge broke, and a great ledge,
Limestone, set my toe high as treetops by the dark edge

Of a gorge, and water hid, grudging and grumbling,
And I saw, in my mind's eye, foam white on
Wet stone, stone wet-black, white water tumbling,
And so went down, and with some fright on
Slick boulders, crossed over. The gorge-depth drew night on,

But high beyond high rock and leaf-lacing, the sky
Showed yet bright, and declivity wooed
My foot by the quietening stream, and so I
Went on, in quiet, through the beech wood:
There, in gold light, where the glade gave, it stood.

The glade was geometric, circular, gold,
No brush or weed breaking that bright gold of leaf-fall.
In the center it stood, absolute and bold
Beyond any heart-hurt, or eye's grief-fall.
Gold-massy the beech stood in that gold light-fall.

*

There was no stir of air, no leaf now gold-falling,
No tooth-stitch of squirrel, or any far fox-bark,
No woodpecker coding, or late jay calling.
Silence: gray-shagged, the great shagbark
Gave forth gold light. There could be no dark.

But of course dark came, and I can't recall
What county it was, for the life of me.
Montgomery, Todd, Christian—I know them all.
Was it even Kentucky or Tennessee?
Is it merely an image that keeps haunting me?

IV Dark Woods

1 Tonight the Woods Are Darkened

Tonight the woods are darkened.
   You have, long back, forgot
What impulse or perturbation
   Had made you rise. You went out

Of the house, where faces and light were,
   To walk, and the night was black.
The dog whined. He tried to follow.
   You picked up some rocks. Rocked him back.

One yelp the brute gave from back there.
   Good. So now you were free
To enter the field and dark there
   Under your heart's necessity.

Under sparse star-gleam a glimmer
   Of pale dust provoked your feet
To pursue the ectoplasmic bisection
   Of the dark field-heave, and to meet,

Yonder where woods massed their darkness,
   A darkness more absolute.
All right: and in shadow the pale dust,
   How soundless, accepted the foot!

✵

Foot trapped in that silken compulsion
    Of dust, and dust-softness, and the pale
Path's glimmer in the field-darkness,
    You moved. Did nerve fail?

Could you stop? No, all's re-enactment.
    Trapped in that *déjà-vu,*
Déjà-fait, déjà-fait, you hear whispers,
    In the dark, say, "Ah." Say: "You, too?"

Was there a field full of folk there,
    Behind you? Threading like mist?
All who, dark-hungry, once had flung forth
    From the house, and now persist

In the field-dark to spy on, then greet you—
    They who now rejoice not, nor grieve,
But yet leer in their spooky connivance,
    Waiting to pluck sleeve?

You wheel now to face them, but nothing
    Is there. Only you. And in starlight,
Beyond the old field and pale cow-track,
    The woods wait. They wait. *All right.*

2 The Dogwood

All right: and with that wry acceptance you follow the cow-track.
Yes, it's dark in the woods, as black as a peddler's pocket.
Cobweb tangles, briar snatches. A sensible man would go back.
A bough finds your face, and one eye grieves in the socket.

Midnight compounds with the peeper. Now whippoorwills speak,
Far off. Then silence. What's that? And something blots star—
By your head velvet air-*whoosh,* a curdle and shudder of wing-creak.
It is only an owl. You go on. You can guess where you are.

For here is the gum-swamp, the slough where you once trapped the weasel.
Here the dead cow was dumped, and by buzzards duly divested.
All taint of mortality's long since wiped clean as a whistle.
Now love vine threads eyehole, God's peace is by violet attested.

The bones are long lost. In green grass the skull waits, has waited:
A cathedral for ants, and at noon, under white dome and transept,
They pass in green gloom, where sunlight's by leaf mitigated,
For leaf of the love vine shuts eyehole, as though the eye slept.

But now it's not noon, it is night, and ant-dark in that cow skull.
And man-dark in the woods. But go on, that's how men survive.
You went on in the dark, your heart tight as a nut in the hull.
Came back in the dark, and home, and throve as men thrive.

✳

But not before you had seen it, sudden at a path-turn,
White-floating in darkness, the dogwood, white bloom in dark air.
Like an ice-break, broke joy; then you felt a strange wrath burn
To strike it, and strike, had a stick been handy in the dark there.

But one wasn't handy, so there on the path then, breath scant,
You stood, you stood there, and oh, could the poor heart's absurd
Cry for wisdom, for wisdom, ever be answered? Triumphant,
All night, the tree glimmered in darkness, and uttered no word.

3 The Hazel Leaf

Tonight the woods are darkened.
   You have forgotten what pain
Had once drawn you forth:
     To remember it might yet be some pain.
     But to forget may, too, be pain.

The hazel leaf falls in autumn.
   It slants athwart the gold air.
Boys come, prompt at nut-fall,
     To shout and kick up the gold leaves there.
     Shouts echo in high hickories not yet bare.

The hazel leaf falls in autumn.
   Boys go, and no voices intrude
Now at dusk-hour. The foot
     Of only the squirrel stirs leaf of this solitude.
     Otherwise, only shadow may now intrude.

The little green snake by the path-side,
   In May, lifts its jeweled head.
It stares, waves the tongue-wisp.
     What it hears on the path is not now your tread.
     But it still stares with lifted head.

*

Yes, your tread's now fainter and farther.
    Years muffle a tread, like grass.
Who passes, strikes; and now goes on.
    The snake waits, head crushed, to be observed by the next to pass.
    He will observe it, and then pass.

Tonight the woods are darkened.
    What other man may go there
Now stares, silent, breath scant,
    Waiting for the white petal to be released in dark air.
    Do not forget you were once there.

V   Country Burying (1919)

A thousand times you've seen that scene:
  Oak grove, bare ground, little white church there,
Bone-white in that light, and through dust-pale green
  Of oak leaf, the steeple pokes up in the bright air.

For it is summer, and once I sat
  At grove-edge beyond the disarray
Of cars in the shade-patch, this way and that.
  They stood patient as mules now in the heat of the day.

Chevrolet, T-Model, a Hudson or two,
  They are waiting like me, and the afternoon glares.
Waiting is all they have come to do.
  What goes on inside is no concern of theirs,

Nor of mine, who have lost a boy's afternoon,
  When summer's so short, and half gone, just to bring
My mother to bury someone she'd scarce known.
  "I respect her," she'd said, but was that enough of a thing?

Who was she? Who knows? I'd not thought to ask it.
  That kind came to town, in buggy or Ford,
Some butter to swap, clutch of eggs in a basket,
  Gnarled hands in black mittens, old face yellow as a gourd.

It's no matter now who lies in the church,
  Where heads bend in duty in sparse rows.
Green miles of tobacco, sun-dazzled, stretch
  Away. Red clay, the road winds, goes on where it goes,

*

And we, too, now go, down the road, where it goes,
  My mother and I, the hole now filled.
Light levels in fields now, dusk crouches in hedgerows,
  As we pass from what is, toward what will be, fulfilled,

And I passed toward voices and the foreign faces,
  Knew dawn in strange rooms, and the heart gropes for center,
But should I come back, come back now where that place is,
  Oak grove, white church, in day-glare a-daze, I might enter.

For what? But enter, and find what I'd guess:
  The odor of varnish, hymnals stacked on a chair,
Light religiously dim by painted paper on window glass,
  And the insistent buzz of a fly lost in shadow, somewhere.

Why doesn't that fly stop buzzing—stop buzzing up there!

V I School Lesson Based on Word of Tragic Death
of Entire Gillum Family

They weren't so bright, or clean, or clever,
  And their noses were sometimes imperfectly blown,
But they always got to school the weather whatever,
  With old lard pail full of fried pie, smoked ham, and corn pone.

Tow hair was thick as a corn-shuck mat.
  They had milky blue eyes in matching pairs,
And barefoot or brogan, when they sat,
  Their toes were the kind that hook round the legs of chairs.

They had adenoids to make you choke,
  And buttermilk breath, and their flannels asteam,
And sat right mannerly while teacher spoke,
  But when book-time came their eyes were glazed and adream.

There was Dollie-May, Susie-May, Forrest, Sam, Brother—
  Thirteen down to eight the stairsteps ran.
They had popped right natural from their fat mother,
  The clabber kind that can catch just by honing after a man.

In town, Gillum stopped you, he'd say: "Say, mister,
  I'll name you what's true fer folks, ever-one.
Human-man ain't much more'n a big blood blister.
  All red and proud-swole, but one good squeeze and he's gone.

*

"Take me, ain't wuth lead and powder to perish,
  Just some spindle bone stuck in a pair of pants,
But a man's got his chaps to love and to cherish,
  And raise up and larn 'em so they kin git their chance."

So mud to the hub, or dust to the hock,
  God his helper, wet or dry,
Old Gillum swore by God and by cock,
  He'd git 'em larned before his own time came to die.

That morning blew up cold and wet,
  All the red-clay road was curdled as curd,
And no Gillums there for the first time yet.
  The morning drones on. Stove spits. Recess. Then the word.

Dollie-May was combing Susie-May's head.
  Sam was feeding, Forrest milking, got nigh through.
Little Brother just sat on the edge of his bed.
  Somebody must have said: "Pappy, now what you aimin' to do?"

An ice pick is a subtle thing.
  The puncture's small, blood only a wisp.
It hurts no more than a bad bee sting.
  When the sheriff got there the school-bread was long burned to a crisp.

In the afternoon silence the chalk would scrape.
  We sat and watched the windowpanes steam,
Blur the old corn field and accustomed landscape.
  Voices came now faint in our intellectual dream.

*

Which shoe—yes, which—was Brother putting on?
   That was something, it seemed, you just had to know.
But nobody knew, all afternoon,
   Though we studied and studied, as hard as we could, to know,

Studying the arithmetic of losses,
   To be prepared when the next one,
By fire, flood, foe, cancer, thrombosis,
   Or Time's slow malediction, came to be undone.

We studied all afternoon, till getting on to sun.
There would be another lesson, but we were too young to take up that one.

V I I Summer Storm (Circa 1916), and God's Grace

Toward sun, the sun flared suddenly red.
   The green of woods was doused to black.
   The cattle bellowed by the haystack.
Redder than ever, red clay was red.
   Up the lane the plowhands came pelting back.

Astride and no saddle, and they didn't care
   If a razor-back mule at a break-tooth trot
   Was not the best comfort a man ever got,
But came huddling on, with jangling gear,
   And the hat that jounced off stayed off, like as not.

In that strange light all distance died.
   You know the world's intensity.
   Field-far, you can read the aphid's eye.
The mole, in his sod, can no more hide,
   And weeps beneath the naked sky.

Past silence, sound insinuates
   Past ear into the inner brain.
   The toad's asthmatic breath is pain,
The cutworm's tooth grinds and grates,
   And the root, in earth, screams, screams again,

But no cloud yet. No wind, though you,
   A half a county off, now spy
   The crow that, laboring zenith-high,
Is suddenly, with wings askew,
   Snatched, and tumbled down the sky.

*

And so you wait. You cannot talk.
  The creek-side willows shudder gray.
  The oak leaves turn the other way,
Gray as fish-belly. Then, with a squawk,
  The henhouse heaves, and flies away,

And darkness rides in on the wind.
  The pitchfork lightning tosses the trees,
  And God gets down on hands and knees
To peer and cackle and commend
  His own sadistic idiocies.

Next morning you stood where the bridge had washed out.
  A drowned cow bobbled down the creek.
  Raw-eyed, men watched. They did not speak.
Till one shrugged, said he guessed he'd make out.
  Then turned, took the woods-path up the creek.

V I I I   Founding Fathers, Nineteenth-Century Style,
Southeast U.S.A.

They were human, they suffered, wore long black coat and gold watch chain.
They stare from daguerreotype with severe reprehension,
Or from genuine oil, and you'd never guess any pain
In those merciless eyes that now remark our own time's sad declension.

Some composed declarations, remembering Jefferson's language.
Knew pose of the patriot, left hand in crook of the spine or
With finger to table, while the right invokes the Lord's just rage.
There was always a grandpa, or cousin at least, who had been a real Signer.

Some were given to study, read Greek in the forest, and these
Longed for an epic to do their own deeds right honor:
Were Nestor by pigpen, in some tavern brawl played Achilles.
In the ring of Sam Houston they found, when he died, one word engraved: *Honor*.

Their children were broadcast, like millet seed flung in a wind-flare.
Wives died, were dropped like old shirts in some corner of country.
Said, "Mister," in bed, the child-bride; hadn't known what to find there;
Wept all next morning for shame; took pleasure in silk; wore the keys to the pantry.

"Will die in these ditches if need be," wrote Bowie, at the Alamo.
And did, he whose left foot, soft-catting, came forward, and breath hissed:
Head back, gray eyes narrow, thumb flat along knife-blade, blade low.
"Great gentleman," said Henry Clay, "and a patriot." Portrait by Benjamin West.
✳

Or take those, the nameless, of whom no portraits remain,
No locket or seal ring, though somewhere, broken and rusted,
In attic or earth, the long Decherd, stock rotten, has lain;
Or the mold-yellow Bible, God's Word, in which, in their strength, they also trusted.

Some wrestled the angel, and took a fall by the corncrib.
Fought the brute, stomp-and-gouge, but knew they were doomed in that glory.
All night, in sweat, groaned; fell at last with spit red and a cracked rib.
How sweet then the tears! Thus gentled, they roved the dark land with the old story.

Some prospered, had black men and acres, and silver on table,
But remembered the owl call, the smell of burnt bear fat on dusk-air.
Loved family and friends, and stood it as long as able—
"But money and women, too much is ruination, am Arkansas-bound." So went there.

One of mine was a land shark, or so the book with scant praise
Denominates him. "A man large and shapeless,
Like a sack of potatoes set on a saddle," it says,
"Little learning but shrewd, not well trusted." Rides thus out of history,
                                        neck fat and napeless.

One fought Shiloh and such, got cranky, would fiddle all night.
The boys nagged for Texas. "God damn it, there's nothing, God damn it,
In Texas"—but took wagons, went, and to prove he was right,
Stayed a year and a day—"hell, nothing in Texas"—had proved it,
                                        came back to black vomit,

*

And died, and they died, and are dead, and now their voices
Come thin, like the last cricket in frost-dark, in grass lost,
With nothing to tell us for our complexity of choices,
But beg us only one word to justify their own old life-cost.

So let us bend ear to them in this hour of lateness,
And what they are trying to say, try to understand,
And try to forgive them their defects, even their greatness,
For we are their children in the light of humanness, and under the shadow
                                                    of God's closing hand.

I X   Foreign Shore, Old Woman, Slaughter of Octopus

What now do the waves say
   To her, the old woman? She wears peasant black,
Alone on the beach, barefoot, and the day
   Withdraws, and she follows her slow track
Among volcanic black boulders, at sea-edge, and does not look back.
Sea-tongue softly utters among boulders by her track.

Saffron-saddening the mountain, the sun
   Sinks, and from sea, black boulder by boulder,
Night creeps. She stops by the boulders, leans on one;
   If from the black shawl she should unfold her
Old hand to the stone, she would find it yet warm, but it will be colder.
What has soft sea-tongue among black boulders told her?

All day there was picnic and laughter,
   Bright eye and hair tossing, white foam and thigh-flash,
And up from some cold coign and dark lair of water,
   Ectoplasmic, snot-gray, the obscene of the life-wish,
Sad tentacles weaving like prayer, eyes wide to glare-horror of day-wash,
The nightmare was spread out on stone. Boys yelled at the knife-flash.

The mountain is black, the sun drops.
   Among the black boulders, slow foam laces white.
Wind stirs, stirs paper of the picnic, stops,
   And agleam in imperial ease, at sky-height,
One gull hangs white in contempt of our human heart, and the night.
Pearl-slime of the slaughter, on black stone, glints in last light.

*

What can the sea tell her,
    That she does not now know, and know how to bear?
She knows, as the sea, that what came will recur,
    And detached in that wisdom, is aware
How grain by slow grain, the last sun heat from sand is expended on night air.
Bare flesh of old foot knows that much, as she stands there.

This is not my country, or tongue,
    And my age not the old woman's age, or sea-age.
I shall go on my errand, and that before long,
    And leave much—but not, sea-darkling, her image,
Which in the day traffic, or as I stand in night dark, may assuage
The mind's pain of logic somewhat, or the heart's rage.

X   Dark Night of the Soul

Far off, two fields away,
Where dark of the river-woods lay,
I saw him divulged into daylight,
And stand to look left and right.
You could guess that quick look aside
Like a creature that knows how to hide
And does not debate pride.

Yes, the owner might come riding
With pistol in pocket, or striding
Along with a stout stick in hand,
To say: "Get the hell off my land!"
And the fellow would understand.

The owner would be justified
To clean him out, hoof-and-hide.
He might set your woods on fire,
Or at least mash down barbed wire.
That's all the excuse you require.

I was twelve, and my property sense
Was defective, though much improved since.
The day, anyway, was a scorcher,
So I didn't get up from the porch or
Even whistle the dogs from the shade
To provoke that flap-jawing parade
Of brute holler and whoop through the heat
To set a tooth in tramp-meat.

Didn't lay down my book, or even shout
Back into the house what was out,
How hedge-skulker and creature of night
And son of pellagra and spite
Now stood in our honest daylight.

There he stood, then slowly moved
One step. Stopped to see if he'd proved
That a man could survive half a minute
Outside the woods and not in it.
Looked back once to black safety of shade,
Then was caught in that great suction made
By the world's bright vacancy.
Was drawn by the world's blank eye.
Moved under the light-dizzy sky.

Far off, he is pin-prick size,
A mote dark in your dazzle of eyes.
He moves without truth or dimension
Across that vast space men should shun.
Lost and faceless and far,
Under light's malevolent stare,
In a painful retardation,
He moves toward what destination,
And so passes over
The enormity of clover.
Is now gone. Has passed over.

Now afternoon, strand by gold strand,
Raveled out, and over the land
Light leveled toward time set
For me to get up and forget
Egypt's arrogant dead

Or that Scaevola whom Rome bred.
Yes, I'd drop my book, and rouse
Myself and leave the house,
To go and round up the cows.

The cows drift up the lane.
White elder blooms by the lane.
I linger, leaf by leaf.
Dust, pale, powders the elder leaf,
And the pale, evening-idle sky
Drains your body light, and dry.
Air moves sweet through your husk under the sky.

But suddenly you are you,
No pale husk the air moves through.
My heart clenched hand-hard as I stood.
The adrenalin tingled my blood.
My lungs made a fish-gasp for air.
Cold prickles ran in my hair.
Beneath elder bloom, the eyes glare.

Couched under elder bloom,
In the honeysuckle he'd made room,
And the white strands regally wreathed
His old head, and the air he breathed
Was heavy with the languishment
Of that too sweet scent.
He was old, rough-grizzled, and spent.

Old and spent, but heaves up his head,
And our eyes thread the single thread
Of the human entrapment, until,
In a voice like a croak from an old well,

He says: "Caint you git on away?"
But I simply can't move away.
He says: "Caint you let a man lay!"

I stared down the dank depth and heard
That croak from cold slime. Then he stirred,
Jerked up, stumbled up in his lair,
Like an old mule snagged on barbed wire.
Jerked free, and a moment stood there.

Then I was left standing alone
To stare down the lane where he'd gone.
He had gone, so I followed the cows
Up yonder toward the house,
There to enter and understand
My plate laid by a loving hand,
And to sleep, but not to understand
That somewhere on the dark land,
Unable to stop or stand,
On a track no man would have planned,
By age, rage, and rejection unmanned,
A bundle of rags in one hand,
His old black felt hat in the other hand,
At last he would understand.

Now his old head, bare,
Moves in the dark air.
It gleams with the absolute and glacial purity of despair.
It moves, and is touched by the unremitting glory of stars high
                                        in the night heavens there.
He moves in joy past contumely of stars or insolent indifference of the dark air.

May we all at last enter into that awfulness of joy he has found there.

X I   Infant Boy at Midcentury

1 When the Century Dragged

When the century dragged, like a great wheel stuck at dead center;
When the wind that had hurled us our half-century sagged now,
And only velleity of air somewhat snidely nagged now,
With no certain commitment to compass, or quarter: then you chose to enter.

You enter an age when the neurotic clock-tick
Of midnight competes with the heart's pulsed assurance of power.
You have entered our world at scarcely its finest hour,
And smile now life's gold Apollonian smile at a sick dialectic.

You enter at the hour when the dog returns to his vomit,
And fear's moonflower spreads, white as girl-thigh, in our dusk of compromise;
When posing for pictures, arms linked, the same smile in their eyes,
Good and Evil, to iron out all differences, stage their meeting at summit.

You come in the year when promises are broken,
And petal fears the late, as fruit the early frost-fall;
When the young expect little, and the old endure total recall,
But discover no logic to justify what they had taken, or forsaken.

But to take and forsake now you're here, and the heart will compress
Like stone when we see that rosy heel learn,
With its first step, the apocalyptic power to spurn
Us, and our works and days, and onward, prevailing, pass

To pause, in high pride of unillusioned manhood,
At the gap that gives on the new century, and land,
And with calm heart and level eye command
That dawning perspective and possibility of human good.

189

2 Modification of Landscape

There will, indeed, be modification of landscape,
And in margin of natural disaster, substantial reduction.
There will be refinement of principle, and purified action,
And expansion, we trust, of the human heart-hope, and hand-scope.

But is it a meanness of spirit and indulgence of spite
To suggest that your fair time, and friends, will mirror our own,
And ourselves, for the flesh will yet grieve on the bone,
And the heart need compensation for its failure to study delight?

Some will take up religion, some discover the virtue of money.
Some will find liberal causes the mask for psychic disturbance.
Some will expiate ego with excessive kindness to servants,
And some make a cult of honor, though having quite little, if any.

Some, hating all humans, will cultivate love for cats,
And some from self-hate will give children a morbid devotion.
Some will glorify friendship, but watch for the slightest motion
Of eyelid, or lip-twitch, and the longed-for betrayal it indicates.

Success for the great will be heart-bread, and the soul's only ease.
For some it will stink, like mackerel shining in moonlight.
At the mere thought of failure some will wet their sheets in the night,
Though some wear it proud as a medal, or manhood's first social disease.

The new age will need the old lies, as our own more than once did;
For death is ten thousand nights—yes, it's only the process
Of accommodating flesh to idea, but there's natural distress
In learning to face Truth's glare-glory, from which our eyes are long hid.

190

3 Brightness of Distance

You will read the official histories—true, no doubt.
Barring total disaster, the record will speak from the shelf.
And if there's disaster, disaster will speak for itself.
So all of our lives will be truth, and the truth vindictively out.

Remember our defects, we give them to you gratis.
But remember that ours is not the worst of times.
Our country's convicted of follies rather than crimes—
We throw out baby with bath, drop the meat in the fire where the fat is.

And in even such stew and stink as Tacitus
Once wrote of, his generals, gourmets, pimps, poltroons,
He found persons of private virtue, the old-fashioned stout ones
Who would bow the head to no blast; and we know that such are yet with us.

He puzzled how virtue found perch past confusion and wrath;
How even Praetorian brutes, blank of love, as of hate,
Proud in their craftsman's pride only, held a last gate,
And died, each back unmarred as though at the barracks bath.

And remember that many among us wish you well;
And once, on a strange shore, an old man, toothless and through,
Groped a hand from the lattice of personal disaster to touch you.
He sat on the sand for an hour; said *ciao, bello,* as evening fell.

And think, as you move past our age that grudges and grieves,
How eyes, purged of envy, will follow your sunlit chance.
Eyes will brighten to follow your brightness and dwindle of distance.
From privacy of fate, eyes will follow, as though from the shadow of leaves.

191

XII Lullaby: Smile in Sleep

Sleep, my son, and smile in sleep.
You will dream the world anew.
Watching you now sleep,
I feel the world's depleted force renew,
Feel the nerve expand and knit,
Feel a rustle in the blood,
Feel wink of warmth and stir of spirit,
As though spring woke in the heart's cold underwood.
The vernal work is now begun.
Sleep, my son.
Sleep, son.

You will see the nestling fall.
Blood flecks grass of the rabbit form.
You will, of course, see all
The world's brute ox-heel wrong, and shrewd hand-harm.
Throats are soft to invite the blade.
Truth invites the journalist's lie.
Love bestowed mourns trust betrayed,
But the heart most mourns its own infidelity.
The greater, then, your obligation.
Dream perfection.
Dream, son.

When the diver leaves the board
To hang at gleam-height against the sky,
Trajectory is toward
An image hung perfect as light in his mind's wide eye.

So your dream will later serve you.
So now, dreaming, you serve me,
And give our hope new patent to
Enfranchise human possibility.
Grace undreamed is grace forgone.
Dream grace, son.
Sleep on.

Dream that sleep is a sunlit meadow
Drowsy with a dream of bees
Threading sun, and the shadow
Where you lie lulled by their sunlit industries.
Let the murmurous bees of sleep
Tread down honey in the honeycomb.
Heart-deep now, your dream will keep
Sweet in that deep comb for time to come.
Dream the sweetness coming on.
Dream, sweet son.
Sleep on.

What if angry vectors veer
Around your sleeping head, and form?
There's never need to fear
Violence of the poor world's abstract storm.
For now you dream Reality.
Matter groans to touch your hand.
Matter lifts now like the sea
Toward that cold moon that is your dream's command.
Dream the power coming on.
Dream, strong son.
Sleep on.

XIII Man in Moonlight

1 Moonlight Observed from Ruined Fortress

Great moon, white-westering past our battlement,
Dark sea offers silver scintillance to your sky,
And not less responsive would my human heart be if I
Had been duly instructed in what such splendors have meant.

I have thought on the question by other sea, other shore:
When you smoothed the sweet Gulf asleep, like a babe at the breast,
When the moon-lashed old freighter banged stars in Atlantic unrest,
When you spangled spume-tangle on black rock, and seals barked at sea-roar.

Décor must be right, of course, for your massive effect,
But a Tennessee stock-pond is not beneath your contempt,
Though its littoral merely a barnyard with cow-pats, unkempt.
Yes, to even a puddle you've been known to pay some respect.

And once on the Cumberland's bluffs I stood at midnight,
With music and laughter behind me, while my eyes
Were trapped in gleam-glory, but the heart's hungry surmise
Faded. So back to the racket and bottle's delight.

Be it sea or a sewer, we know you have never much cared
What sort of excuse, just so you may preen and prink,
With vulgarities to make Belasco blink
And tricks that even Houdini wouldn't have dared.

Now with that old, anguishing virtuosity
You strike our cliff, and then lean on to Carthage.
We stand on the crumbling stone and ruins of rage,
To watch your Tyrrhenian silver prank the sea.

*

194

And so we enact again the compulsive story,
Knowing of course the end—and ah, how soon—
But caught in that protocol of plenilune
And that werewolf thirst to drink the blood of glory.

We stare, we stare, but will not stare for long.
You will not tell us what we need to know.
Our feet soon go the way that they must go,
In diurnal dust and heat, and right and wrong.

2 Walk by Moonlight in Small Town

Through the western window full fell moonlight.
It must have waked me where I lay.
Room objects swam in that spooky day.
I rose, dressed, walked the summer night,
As long years back I had moved in that compulsive light.

Lawns green by day now shimmered like frost.
Shadow, beast-black, in porches lurked.
On house fronts, windowpanes moon-smirked.
Past supper, paper read, lawn hosed,
How white, in the depth of dark rooms now, faces reposed.

Down Main Street, the window dummies blessed,
With lifted hand and empty stare,
The glimmering emptiness of air,
As though lunatically to attest
What hope the daylight heart might reasonably have possessed.

Three boxcars slept, as quiet as cows.
They were so tired, they'd been so far.
SP and *Katy, L & N R R*—
After bumble and bang, and where God knows,
They'd cracked the rust of a weed-rank spur, for this pale repose.

Long, long ago, at night, up that track,
I had watched the Pullmans flash and fade,
Then heard, in new quiet, the beat my heart made.
But every ticket's round-trip; now back,
I stood and again watched night-distance flee up that empty track.

✳

I crossed the track, walked up the rise.
The school building hulked, ugly as day.
Beyond, the night fields fell away.
Building and grounds had shrunk in size,
And that predictable fact seemed pitiful to my eyes.

And pitiful was the moon-bare ground.
Dead grass, the gravel, earth ruined and raw—
It had not changed. And then I saw
That children were playing, with no sound.
They ceased their play, then quiet as moonlight, drew, slow, around.

Their eyes were fixed on me, and I
Now tried, face by pale face, to find
The names that haunted in my mind.
Each small, upgazing face would lie
Sweet as a puddle, and silver-calm, to the night sky.

But something grew in their pale stare:
Not reprobation or surprise,
Nor even forgiveness in their eyes,
But a humble question dawning there,
From face to face, like beseechment dawning on empty air.

Might a man but know his Truth, and might
He live so that life, by moon or sun,
In dusk or dawn, would be all one—
Then never on a summer night
Need he stand and shake in that cold blaze of Platonic light.

3 Lullaby: Moonlight Lingers

Moonlight lingers down the air.
Moonlight marks the window-square
As I stand and watch you sleep.
I hear the rustle where
The sea stirs sweet and sighs in its silvered sleep.
My son, sleep deep.
Sleep deep, son, and dream how moonlight
Unremitting, whitely, whitely, unpetals down the night.
As you sleep, now moonlight
Mollifies the mountain's rigor,
Laves the olive leaf to silver,
And black on the moon-pale trunk of the olive
Prints the shadow of an olive leaf.
Sleep, let moonlight give
That dark secondary definition to the olive leaf.
Sleep, son, past grief.

Now I close my eyes and see
Moonlight white on a certain tree.
It was a big white oak near a door
Familiar, long back, to me,
But now years unseen, and my foot enters there no more.
My son, sleep deep.
Sleep deep, son, and let me think
How a summer lane glimmers in moonlight to the cedar woods' dark brink.
Sleep, and let me now think
Of moon-frost white on the black boughs of cedar,

White moon-rinse on meadow, whiter than clover,
And at moon-dark stone, how water woke
In a wink of glory, then slid on to sleep.
Sleep, let this moon provoke
Moonlight more white on that landscape lost in the heart's homely deep.
Son, past grief, sleep.

Moonlight falls on sleeping faces.
It fell in far times and other places.
Moonlight falls on your face now,
And now in memory's stasis
I see moonlight mend an old man's Time-crossed brow.
My son, sleep deep,
For moonlight will not stay.
Now moves to seek that empty pillow, a hemisphere away.
Here, then, you'll be waking to the day.
Those who died, died long ago,
Faces you will never know,
Voices you will never hear—
Though your father heard them in the night,
And yet, sometimes, I can hear
Their utterance like the rustling tongue of a pale tide in moonlight:
Sleep, son. Good night.

X I V   Mad Young Aristocrat on Beach

He sits in blue trunks on the sand, and children sing.
Their voices are crystal and sad, and tinkle in sunlight.
Their voices are crystal, and the tinkling
Of sadness, like gold ants, crawls on his quivering heart in its midnight.
And the sea won't be still, won't be still,
In that freaking and fracture and dazzle of light.
Yes, somebody ought to take steps and stop it.
It's high time that somebody did, and he thinks that he will.
Why, it's simple, it's simple, just get a big mop and mop it,
Till it's dry as a bone—you sea, you *cretino,* be still!
But he's tired, he is tired, and wants only sleep.
Oh, Lord, let us pray that the children stop singing before he begins to weep.

If he wept, we just couldn't bear it, but look, he is smiling!
He ponders how charming it is to smile, and magnanimous.
And his smile, indeed, is both sweet and beguiling,
And joy floods his heart now like hope, to replace that old dark animus.
So look! at the great concert grand,
He is bowing, and bowing, and smiling now on us,
And smiles at the sea, at the sea's bright applause—
But fame, ah, how sad! Again he sits on the sand,
And thinks how all human rewards are but gauds and gewgaws,
And lets sand, grain by grain, like history slip from his hand.
But his mother once said that his smile was sweet.
Curse the bitch, it is power man wants, and like a black cloud now mounts to his feet.

✳

He is young and sun-brown and tall and well formed, and he knows it.
He will swim in the sea, the water will break to his will.
Now emerging on shore, he is lethal, he shows it.
Yes, let them beware that brute jaw-jut and eye cold now and still.
And let him beware, beware—
That brother, the elder, who comes to the title.
But a title, *merde!* he will marry a passport,
And dollars, of course—he has blood, though he isn't the heir.
Then sudden as death, a thought stops him chillingly short:
Mais l'Amérique, merde! why it's full of Americans there.
So closes his eyes, longs for home, longs for bed.
Ah, that sweet-haunched new housemaid! But knows he can't get her except
in the dark of his head.

So thinks of a whore he once had: she was dull as a sow,
And not once, never once, showed affection. He thinks he will cry.
Then thinks, with heart sweet, he'll be dead soon now,
And opens his eyes to the blaze and enormousness of the sky.
And we watch him, we watch him, and we
Are lonely, are lonely as death, though we try
To love him, but can't, for we sit on the sand,
And eyes throb at the merciless brilliance and bicker of sea,
While sand, grain by grain, like our history, slips from his hand.
We should love him, because his flesh suffers for you and for me,
As our own flesh should suffer for him, and for all
Who will never come to the title, and be loved for themselves, at innocent nightfall.

X V   Dragon Country: To Jacob Boehme

This is the dragon's country, and these his own streams.
The slime on the railroad rails is where he has crossed the track.
On a frosty morning, that field mist is where his great turd steams,
And there are those who have gone forth and not come back.

I was only a boy when Jack Simms reported the first depredation,
What something had done to his hog pen. They called him a God-damn liar.
Then said it must be a bear, after some had viewed the location,
With fence rails, like matchwood, splintered, and earth a bloody mire.

But no bear had been seen in the county in fifty years, they knew.
It was something to say, merely that, for people compelled to explain
What, standing in natural daylight, they agreed couldn't be true;
And saying the words, a man felt in the chest a constrictive pain.

At least, some admitted this later, when things had got to the worst—
When, for instance, they found in the woods the wagon turned on its side,
Mules torn from trace chains, and you saw how the harness had burst.
Spectators averted the face from the spot where the teamster had died.

But that was long back, in my youth, just the first of case after case.
The great hunts fizzled. You followed the track of disrepair,
Ruined fence, blood-smear, brush broken, but came in the end to a place
With weed unbent and leaf calm—and nothing, nothing, was there.

So what, in God's name, could men think when they couldn't bring to bay
That belly-dragging earth-evil, but found that it took to air?
Thirty-thirty or buckshot might fail, but then at least you could say
You had faced it—assuming, of course, that you had survived the affair.

*

We were promised troops, the Guard, but the Governor's skin got thin
When up in New York the papers called him Saint George of Kentucky.
Yes, even the Louisville reporters who came to Todd County would grin.
Reporters, though rarely, still come. No one talks. They think it unlucky.

If a man disappears—well, the fact is something to hide.
The family says, gone to Akron, or up to Ford, in Detroit.
When we found Jebb Johnson's boot, with the leg, what was left, inside,
His mother said, no, it's not his. So we took it out to destroy it.

Land values are falling, no longer do lovers in moonlight go.
The rabbit, thoughtless of air gun, in the nearest pasture cavorts.
Now certain fields go untended, the local birth rate goes low.
The coon dips his little black paw in the riffle where he nightly resorts.

Yes, other sections have problems somewhat different from ours.
Their crops may fail, bank rates rise, loans at rumor of war be called,
But we feel removed from maneuvers of Russia, or other great powers,
And from much ordinary hope we are now disenthralled.

The Catholics have sent in a mission, Baptists report new attendance.
All that's off the point! We are human, and the human heart
Demands language for reality that has not the slightest dependence
On desire, or need—and in church fools pray only that the Beast depart.

But if the Beast were withdrawn now, life might dwindle again
To the ennui, the pleasure, and the night sweat, known in the time before
Necessity of truth had trodden the land, and our hearts, to pain,
And left, in darkness, the fearful glimmer of joy, like a spoor.

203

X V I Ballad of a Sweet Dream of Peace

1 And Don't Forget Your Corset Cover, Either

And why, in God's name, is that elegant bureau
Standing out here in the woods and dark?
Because, in God's name, it would create a furor
If such a Victorian piece were left in the middle of Central Park,
To corrupt the morals of young and old
With its marble top and drawer pulls gilt gold
And rosewood elaborately scrolled,
And would you, in truth, want your own young sister to see it in the Park?
But she knows all about it, her mother has told her,
And besides, these days, she is getting much older,
And why, in God's name, is that bureau left in the woods?
All right, I'll tell you why.
It has as much right there as you or I,
For the woods are God's temple, and even a bureau has moods.
But why, in God's name, is that elegant bureau left all alone in the woods?

It is left in the woods for the old lady's sake,
For there's privacy here for a household chore,
And Lord, I can't tell you the time it can take
To apply her own mixture of beeswax and newt-oil to bring out the gloss once more.
For the poor old hands move slower each night,
And can't manage to hold the cloth very tight,
And it's hard without proper light.
But why, in God's name, all this privacy for a simple household chore?

In God's name, sir! would you simply let
Folks see how naked old ladies can get?
Then let the old bitch buy some clothes like other folks do.
She once had some clothes, I am told,
But they're long since ruined by the damp and mold,
And the problem is deeper when bones let the wind blow through.
Besides it's not civil to call her a bitch—and her your own grandma, too.

2 Keepsakes

Oh, what brings her out in the dark and night?
She has mislaid something, just what she can't say,
But something to do with the bureau, all right.
Then why, in God's name, does she polish so much, and not look

in a drawer right away?

Every night, in God's name, she does look there,
But finds only a Book of Common Prayer,
A ribbon-tied lock of gold hair,
A bundle of letters, some contraceptives, and an orris-root sachet.
Well, what is the old fool hunting for?
Oh, nothing, oh, nothing that's in the top drawer,
For that's left by late owners who had their own grief to withstand,
And she tries to squinch and frown
As she peers at the Prayer Book upside down,
And the contraceptives are something she can't understand,
And oh, how bitter the tears she sheds, with some stranger's old letters in hand!

You're lying, you're lying, she can't shed a tear!
Not with eyeballs gone, and the tear ducts, too.
You are trapped in a vulgar error, I fear,
For asleep in the bottom drawer is a thing that may prove instructive to you:
Just an old-fashioned doll with a china head,
And a cloth body naked and violated
By a hole through which sawdust once bled,
But drop now by drop, on a summer night, from her heart it is treacle bleeds through.

206

In God's name, what!—Do I see her eyes move?
Of course, and she whispers, "I died for love,"
And your grandmother whines like a dog in the dark and shade,
For she's hunting somebody to give
Her the life they had promised her she would live,
And I shudder to think what a stink and stir will be made
When some summer night she opens the drawer and finds that poor self she'd mislaid.

3 Go It, Granny—Go It, Hog!

Out there in the dark, what's that horrible chomping?
Oh, nothing, just hogs that forage for mast,
And if you call, "Hoo-pig!" they'll squeal and come romping,
For they'll know from your voice you're the boy who slopped them
                                                in dear, dead days long past.
Any hogs that I slopped are long years dead,
And eaten by somebody and evacuated,
So it's simply absurd, what you said.
You fool, poor fool, all Time is a dream, and we're all one Flesh, at last,
And the hogs know that, and that's why they wait,
Though tonight the old thing is a little bit late,
But they're mannered, these hogs, as they wait for her creaky old tread.
Polite, they will sit in a ring,
Till she finishes work, the poor old thing:
Then old bones get knocked down with a clatter to wake up the dead,
And it's simply absurd how loud she can scream with no shred of a tongue
                                                in her head.

208

4 Friends of the Family, or Bowling a Sticky Cricket

Who else, in God's name, comes out in these woods?
Old friends of the family, whom you never saw,
Like yon cranky old coot, who mumbles and broods,
With yachting cap, rusty frock coat, and a placard proclaiming, "I am the Law!"
What makes him go barefoot at night in God's dew?
In God's name, you idiot, so would you
If you'd suffered as he had to
When expelled from his club for the horrible hobby that taught him the nature of law.
They learned that he drowned his crickets in claret.
The club used cologne, and so couldn't bear it.
But they drown them in claret in Buckingham Palace!
Fool, law is inscrutable, so
Barefoot in dusk and dew he must go,
And at last each cries out in a dark stone-glimmering place,
"I have heard the voice in the dark, seeing not who utters. Show me Thy face!"

5 You Never Knew Her Either, Though You Thought You Did

Why now, in God's name, is her robe de nuit
So torn and bedraggled, and what is that stain?
It's only dried blood, in God's name, that you see.
But why does she carry that leaf in her hand? Will you try, in God's name, to explain?
It's a burdock leaf under which she once found
Two toads in coitu on the bare black ground,
So now she is nightly bound
To come forth to the woods to embrace a thorn tree, to try to understand pain,
And then wipes the blood on her silken hair,
And cries aloud, "Oh, we need not despair,
For I bleed, oh, I bleed, and God lives!" And the heart may stir
Like water beneath wind's tread
That wanders whither it is not said.
Oh, I almost forgot—will you please identify her?
She's the afternoon one who to your bed came, lip damp, the breath like myrrh.

6 I Guess You Ought to Know Who You Are

Could that be a babe crawling there in night's black?
Why, of course, in God's name, and birth-blind, but you'll see
How to that dead chestnut he'll crawl a straight track,
Then give the astonishing tongue of a hound with a coon treed up in a tree.
Well, who is the brat, and what's he up to?
He's the earlier one that they thought would be you,
And perhaps, after all, it was true,
For it's hard in these matters to tell sometimes. *But look, in God's name, I am me!*
If you are, there's the letter a hog has in charge,
With a gold coronet and your own name writ large,
And in French, most politely, "Répondez s'il vous plaît."
Now don't be alarmed we are late.
What's time to a hog? We'll just let them wait.
But for when you are ready, our clients usually say
That to shut the eyes tight and get down on the knees is the quickest and easiest way.

7 Rumor Unverified Stop Can You Confirm Stop

Yes, clients report it the tidiest way,
For the first time at least, when all is so strange
And the helpers get awkward sometimes with delay.
But later, of course, you can try other methods that fancy suggests you arrange.
There are clients, in fact, who, when ennui gets great,
Will struggle, or ingeniously irritate
The helpers to acts I won't state:
For Reality's all, and to seek it, some welcome, at whatever cost, any change.
But speaking of change, there's a rumor astir
That the woods are sold, and the purchaser
Soon comes, and if credulity's not now abused,
Will, on this property, set
White foot-arch familiar to violet,
And heel that, smiting stone, is not what is bruised,
And subdues to sweetness the pathside garbage, or thing body had refused.

XVII Boy's Will, Joyful Labor Without Pay, and Harvest Home (1918)

1 Morning

By breakfast time the bustle's on.
In the field the old red thresher clatters.
The old steam tractor shakes and batters.
Sweat pops already in the hot sun.
The dogs are barking, mad as hatters.

You bolt your oatmeal, up and go.
The world is panting, the world won't wait.
All energy's unregenerate.
Blood can't abide the status quo.
You run as far as the front gate,

Then stop. For when your hope is displayed
To wait you, you must feast the eye
An instant on possibility,
Before finite constriction is made
To our pathos of rapacity.

2 Work

The hand that aches for the pitchfork heft
Heaves a sheaf from the shock's rich disrepair.
The wagoner snags it in mid-air,
Says, "Boy, save yore strength, 'fore you got none left,"
And grins, then wipes the sweat from his hair.

3 The Snake

Daylong, light, gold, leans on the land.
You stoke the tractor. You *gee* and *haw*.
You feed the thresher's gap-toothed maw.
Then on a load-top, high, you stand
And see your shadow, black as law,

Stretch far now on the gold stubble.
By now breath's short. Sweat stings the eyes.
Blue denim is sweat-black at the thighs.
If you make a joke, you waste your trouble.
In that silence the shout rings with surprise.

When you wreck a shock, the spot below
Is damp and green with a vernal gloom.
Field mouse or rabbit flees its doom,
And you scarcely notice how they go.
But a black snake rears big in his ruined room.

Defiant, tall in that blast of day,
Now eye for eye, he swaps his stare.
His outrage glitters on the air.
Men shout, ring around. He can't get away.
Yes, they are men, and a stone is there.

Against the wounded evening matched,
Snagged high on a pitchfork tine, he will make
Slow arabesques till the bullbats wake.
An old man, standing stooped, detached,
Spits once, says, "Hell, just another snake."

4 Hands Are Paid

The thresher now has stopped its racket.
It waits there small by the stack it has made.
The work is done, the hands are paid.
The silver dollar's in the sweat-cold pocket,
And the shirt sticks cold to the shoulder blade.

Out of the field, the way it had come,
Dragging the thresher's list and bumble,
The tractor now, a-clank, a-shamble,
Grunts down the pike, the long way home.
In dusk, to water now, mules, slow, amble.

The dollar glints on the mantel shelf.
By the coal-oil lamp the man leans his head
Over fried sowbelly and cold corn bread.
He's too sleepy now to wash himself.
Kicks off his brogans. Gets to bed.

The bullbat has come, long back, and gone.
White now, the evening star hangs to preside
Over woods and dark water and far countryside.
The little blood that smeared the stone
Dropped in the stubble, has long since dried.

The springs of the bed creak now, and settle.
The overalls hang on the back of a chair
To stiffen, slow, as the sweat gets drier.
Far, under a cedar, the tractor's metal
Surrenders last heat to the night air.

*
216

In the cedar dark a white moth drifts.
The mule's head, at the barn-lot bar,
Droops sad and saurian under night's splendor.
In the star-pale field, the propped pitchfork lifts
Its burden, hung black, to the white star,

And the years go by like a breath, or eye-blink,
And all history lives in the head again,
And I shut my eyes and I see that scene,
And name each item, but cannot think
What, in their urgency, they must mean,

But know, even now, on this foreign shore,
In blaze of sun and the sea's stare,
A heart-stab blessed past joy or despair,
As I see, in the mind's dark, once more,
That field, pale, under starlit air.

X V I I I   Lullaby: A Motion Like Sleep

Under the star and beech-shade braiding,
Past the willow's dim solicitudes,
Past hush of oak-dark and stone's star-glinted upbraiding,
Water moves, in a motion like sleep,
Along the dark edge of the woods.
So, son, now sleep.

Sleep, and feel how now, at woods-edge,
The water, wan, moves under starlight,
Before it finds that dark of its own deepest knowledge,
And will murmur, in motion like sleep,
In that leaf-dark languor of night.
So, son, sleep deep.

Sleep, and dream how deep and dreamless
The covered courses of blood are:
And blood, in a motion like sleep, moves, gleamless,
By alleys darkened deep now
In leafage of no star.
So, son, sleep now.

Sleep, for sleep and stream and blood-course
Are a motion with one name,
And all that flows finds end but in its own source,
And a circuit of motion like sleep,
And will go as once it came.
So, son, now sleep

*

Till the clang of cock-crow, and dawn's rays,
Summon your heart and hand to deploy
Their energies and to know, in the excitement of day-blaze,
How like a wound, and deep,
Is Time's irremediable joy.
So, son, now sleep.

From SELECTED POEMS
1923–1943

THE BALLAD OF BILLIE POTTS

(When I was a child I heard this story from an old lady who was a relative of mine. The scene, according to her version, was in the section of Western Kentucky known as "Between the Rivers," the region between the Cumberland and the Tennessee. The name of Bardstown in the present account refers to Bardstown, Kentucky, where the first race track west of the mountains was laid out late in the eighteenth century.)

Big Billie Potts was big and stout
In the land between the rivers.
His shoulders were wide and his gut stuck out
Like a croker of nubbins and his holler and shout
Made the bob-cat shiver and the black-jack leaves shake
In the section between the rivers.
He would slap you on your back and laugh.

Big Billie had a wife, she was dark and little
In the land between the rivers,
And clever with her wheel and clever with her kettle,
But she never said a word and when she sat
By the fire her eyes worked slow and narrow like a cat.
Nobody knew what was in her head.

They had a big boy with fuzz on his chin
So tall he ducked the door when he came in,
A clabber-headed bastard with snot in his nose
And big red wrists hanging out of his clothes
And a whicker when he laughed where his father had a bellow
In the section between the rivers.
They called him Little Billie.
He was their darling.

(It is not hard to see the land, what it was.
Low hills and oak. The fetid bottoms where
The slough uncoiled and in the tangled cane,

223

Where no sun comes, the muskrat's astute face
Was lifted to the yammering jay; then dropped.
A cabin where the shagbark stood and the
Magnificent tulip-tree; both now are gone.
But the land is there, and as you top a rise,
Beyond you all the landscape steams and simmers
—The hills, now gutted, red, cane-brake and black-jack yet.
The oak leaf steams under the powerful sun.
"Mister, is this the right road to Paducah?"
The red face, seamed and gutted like the hill,
Slow under time, and with the innocent savagery
Of Time, the bleared eyes rolling, answers from
Your dream: "They names it so, but I ain't bin.")

Big Billie was the kind who laughed but could spy
The place for a ferry where folks would come by.
He built an inn and folks bound West
Hitched their horses there to take their rest
And grease the gall and grease the belly
And jaw and spit under the trees
In the section between the rivers.
Big Billie said: "Git down, friend, and take yore ease!"
He would slap you on your back and set you at his table.

(Leaning and slow, you see them move
In massive passion colder than any love:
Their lips move but you do not hear the words,
Nor trodden twig nor fluted irony of birds,
Nor hear the rustle of the heart
That, heave and settle, gasp and start,
Heaves like a fish in the ribs' dark basket borne
West from the great water's depth whence it was torn.

*

224

Their names are like the leaves, but are forgot
—The slush and swill of the world's great pot
That foamed at the Appalachian lip, and spilled
Like quicksilver across green baize, the unfulfilled
Disparate glitter, gleam, wild symptom, seed
Flung in the long wind: silent, they proceed
Past meadow, salt-lick, and the lyric swale;
Enter the arbor, shadow of trees, fade, fail.)

Big Billie was sharp at swap and trade
And could smell the nest where the egg was laid.
He could read and cipher and they called him squire,
And he added up his money while he sat by the fire,
And sat in the shade while folks sweated and strove,
For he was the one who fatted and throve
In the section between the rivers.
"Thank you kindly, sir," Big Billie would say
When the man in the black coat paid him at streak of day
And swung to the saddle, was ready to go,
And rode away and didn't know
That he was already as good as dead,
For at midnight the message had been sent ahead:
"Man in black coat, riding bay mare with star."

(There was a beginning but you cannot see it.
There will be an end but you cannot see it.
They will not turn their faces to you though you call,
Who pace a logic merciless as light,
Whose law is their long shadow on the grass,
Sun at the back; who pace, pass,
And passing nod in that glacial delirium
While the tight sky shudders like a drum

And speculation rasps its idiot nails
Across the dry slate where you did the sum.

The answer is in the back of the book but the page is gone.
And Grandma told you to tell the truth but she is dead.
And heedless, their hairy faces fixed
Beyond your call or question now, they move
Under the infatuate weight of their wisdom,
Precious but for the preciousness of their burden,
Sainted and sad and sage as the hairy ass, these who bear
History like bound faggots, with stiff knees;
And breathe the immaculate climate where
The lucent leaf is lifted, lank beard fingered, by no breeze,
Rapt in the fabulous complacency of fresco, vase, or frieze:

And the testicles of the fathers hang down like old lace.)

Little Billie was full of vinegar
And full of sap as a maple tree
And full of tricks as a lop-eared pup,
So one night when the runner didn't show up,
Big Billie called Little and said, "Saddle up,"
And nodded toward the man who was taking his sup
With his belt unlatched and his feet to the fire.
Big Billie said, "Give Amos a try,
Fer this feller takes the South Fork and Amos'll be nigher
Than Baldy or Buster, and Amos is sly
And slick as a varmint, and I don't deny
I lak business with Amos, fer he's one you kin trust
In the section between the rivers,
And it looks lak they's mighty few.
Amos will split up fair and square."
*

Little Billie had something in his clabber-head
By way of brains, and he reckoned he knew
How to skin a cat or add two and two.
So long before the sky got red
Over the land between the rivers,
He hobbled his horse back in the swamp
And squatted on his hams in the morning dew and damp
And scratched his stomach and grinned to think
How Pap would be proud and Mammy glad
To know what a thriving boy they had.
He always was a good boy to his darling Mammy.

(Think of yourself riding away from the dawn,
Think of yourself and the unnamed ones who had gone
Before, riding, who rode away from *goodbye, goodbye,*
And toward *hello,* toward Time's unwinking eye;
And like the cicada had left, at cross-roads or square,
The old shell of self, thin, ghostly, translucent, light as air;
At dawn riding into the curtain of unwhispering green,
Away from the vigils and voices into the green
World, land of the innocent bough, land of the leaf.
Think of your face green in the submarine light of the leaf.

Or think of yourself crouched at the swamp-edge:
Dawn-silence past last owl-hoot and not yet at day-verge
First bird-stir, titmouse or drowsy warbler not yet.
You touch the grass in the dark and your hand is wet.
Then light: and you wait for the stranger's hoofs on the soft trace,
And under the green leaf's translucence the light bathes your face.

Think of yourself at dawn: Which one are you? What?)
❄

Little Billie heard hoofs on the soft grass,
But squatted and let the rider pass,
For he wouldn't waste good lead and powder
Just to make the slough-fish and swamp-buzzards prouder
In the land between the rivers.
But he saw the feller's face and thanked his luck
It was the one Pap said was fit to pluck.
So he got on his horse and cantered up the trace.
Called, "Hi thar!" and the stranger watched him coming,
And sat his mare with a smile on his face,
Just watching Little Billie and smiling and humming.
Little Billie rode up and the stranger said,
"Why, bless my heart, if it ain't Little Billie!"

"Good mornen," said Billie, and said, "My Pap
Found somethen you left and knowed you'd be missen,
And Pap don't want nuthen not proper his'n."
But the stranger didn't do a thing but smile and listen
Polite as could be to what Billie said.
But he must have had eyes in the side of his head
As they rode along beside the slough
In the land between the rivers,
Or guessed what Billie was out to do,
For when Billie said, "Mister, I've brung it to you,"
And reached his hand for it down in his britches,
The stranger just reached his own hand, too.

"Boom!" Billie's gun said, and the derringer, "Bang!"
"Oh, I'm shot!" Billie howled and grabbed his shoulder.
"Not bad," said the stranger, "for you're born to hang,
But I'll save some rope 'fore you're a minute older
If you don't high-tail to your honest Pap

In the section between the rivers."
Oh, Billie didn't tarry and Billie didn't linger,
For Billie didn't trust the stranger's finger
And didn't admire the stranger's face
And didn't like the climate of the place,
So he turned and high-tailed up the trace,
With blood on his shirt and snot in his nose
And pee in his pants, for he'd wet his clothes,
And the stranger just sits and admires how he goes,
And says, "Why, that boy would do right well back on the Bardstown track!"

"You fool!" said his Pap, but his Mammy cried
To see the place where the gore-blood dried
Round the little hole in her darling's hide.
She wiped his nose and patted his head,
But Pappy barred the door and Pappy said,
"Two hundred in gold's in my money belt,
And take the roan and the brand-new saddle
And stop yore blubberen and skeedaddle,
And next time you try and pull a trick
Fer God's sake don't talk but do it quick."

So Little Billie took his leave
And left his Mammy there to grieve
And left his Pappy in Old Kaintuck
And headed West to try his luck,
For it was Roll, Missouri,
It was Roll, roll, Missouri.
And he was gone nigh ten long year
And never sent word to give his Pappy cheer
Nor wet pen in ink for his Mammy dear.
For Little Billie never was much of a hand with a pen-staff.

*

229

(There is always another country and always another place.
There is always another name and another face.
And the name and the face are you, and you
The name and the face, and the stream you gaze into
Will show the adoring face, show the lips that lift to you
As you lean with the implacable thirst of self,
As you lean to the image which is yourself,
To set the lip to lip, fix eye on bulging eye,
To drink not of the stream but of your deep identity,
But water is water and it flows,
Under the image on the water the water coils and goes
And its own beginning and its end only the water knows.

There are many countries and the rivers in them
—Cumberland, Tennessee, Ohio, Colorado, Pecos, Little Big Horn,
And Roll, Missouri, roll.
But there is only water in them.

And in the new country and in the new place
The eyes of the new friend will reflect the new face
And his mouth will speak to frame
The syllables of the new name
And the name is you and is the agitation of the air
And is the wind and the wind runs and the wind is everywhere.

The name and the face are you.
The name and the face are always new
And they are you.
Are new.

For they have been dipped in the healing flood.
For they have been dipped in the redeeming blood.
For they have been dipped in Time.

For Time is always the new place,
And no-place.
For Time is always the new name and the new face,
And no-name and no-face.

For Time is motion
For Time is innocence
For Time is West.)

Oh, who is coming along the trace,
Whistling along in the late sunshine,
With a big black hat above his big red face
And a long black coat that swings so fine?
Oh, who is riding along the trace
Back to the land between the rivers,
With a big black beard growing down to his guts
And silver mountings on his pistol-butts
And a belt as broad as a saddle-girth
And a look in his eyes like he owned the earth?
And meets a man riding up the trace
And squints right sharp and scans his face
And says, "Durn, if it ain't Joe Drew!"
"I reckin it's me," says Joe and gives a spit,
"But whupped if I figger how you knows it,
Fer if I'm Joe, then who air you?"
And the man with the black beard says: "Why, I'm Little Billie!"
And Joe Drew says: "Wal, I'll be whupped."

"Be whupped," Joe said, "and whar you goen?"
"Oh, just visiten back whar I done my growen
In the section between the rivers,
Fer I bin out West and taken my share
And I reckin my luck helt out fer fair,

So I done come home," Little Billie said,
"To see my folks if they ain't dead."
"Ain't dead," Joe answered, and shook his head,
"But that's the best a man kin say,
Fer it looked lak when you went away
You taken West yore Pappy's luck."
Little Billie jingled his pockets and said: "Ain't nuthen wrong with my luck."

And said: "Wal, I'll be gitten on home,
But after yore supper why don't you come
And we'll open a jug and you tell me the news
In the section between the rivers.
But not too early, fer it's my aim
To git me some fun 'fore they know my name,
And tease 'em and fun 'em, fer you never guessed
I was Little Billie what went out West."
And Joe Drew said: "Durn if you always wasn't a hand to git yore fun."

(Over the plain, over mountain and river, drawn,
Wanderer with slit-eyes adjusted to distance,
Drawn out of distance, drawn from the great plateau
Where the sky heeled in the unsagging wind and the cheek burned,
Who stood beneath the white peak that glimmered like a dream,
And spat, and it was morning and it was morning.
You lay among the wild plums and the kildees cried.
You lay in the thicket under the new leaves and the kildees cried,
For you all luck, for all the astuteness of your heart,
And would not stop and would not stop
And the clock ticked all night long in the furnished room
And would not stop
And the *El*-train passed on the quarters with a whish like a terrible broom
And would not stop

And there is always the sound of breathing in the next room
And it will not stop
And the waitress says, "Will that be all, sir, will that be all?"
And will not stop
For nothing is ever all and nothing is ever all,
For all your experience and your expertness of human vices and of valor
At the hour when the ways are darkened.

Though your luck held and the market was always satisfactory,
Though the letter always came and your lovers were always true,
Though you always received the respect due to your position,
Though your hand never failed of its cunning and your glands always
                                        thoroughly knew their business,
Though your conscience was easy and you were assured of your innocence,
You became gradually aware that something was missing from the picture,
And upon closer inspection exclaimed: "Why, I'm not in it at all!"
Which was perfectly true.

Therefore you tried to remember when you had last had
Whatever it was you had lost,
And you decided to retrace your steps from that point,
But it was a long way back.
It was, nevertheless, absolutely essential to make the effort,
And since you had never been a man to be deterred by difficult circumstances,
You came back.
For there is no place like home.)

He joked them and teased them and he had his fun
And they never guessed that he was the one
Had been Mammy's darling and Pappy's joy
When he was a great big whickering boy
In the land between the rivers.
He jingled his pockets and took his sop

And patted his belly which was full nigh to pop
And wiped the buttermilk out of his beard
And took his belch and up and reared
Back from the table and cocked his chair
And said: "Old man, ain't you got any fresh drinken water, this here
              ain't fresher'n a hoss puddle?"
And the old woman said: "Pappy, take the young gentleman
         down to the spring so he kin git it good and fresh?"
The old woman gave the old man a straight look.
She gave him the bucket but it was not empty but it was not water.

The stars are shining and the meadow is bright
But under the trees is dark and night
In the land between the rivers.
The leaves hang down in the dark of the trees,
And there is the spring in the dark of the trees,
And there is the spring as black as ink,
And one star in it caught through a chink
Of the leaves that hang down in the dark of the trees.
The star is there but it does not wink.
Little Billie gets down on his knees
And props his hands in the same old place
To sup the water at his ease;
And the star is gone but there is his face.
"Just help yoreself," Big Billie said;
Then set the hatchet in his head.
They went through his pockets and they buried him in the dark of the trees.
"I figgered he was a ripe 'un," the old man said.
"Yeah, but you wouldn't done nuthen hadn't bin fer me," the old woman said.

(The reflection is shadowy and the form not clear,
For the hour is late, and scarcely a glimmer comes here

234

Under the leaf, the bough, in its innocence dark;
And under your straining face you can scarcely mark
The darkling gleam of your face little less than the water dark.

But perhaps what you lost was lost in the pool long ago
When childlike you lost it and then in your innocence rose to go
After kneeling, as now, with your thirst beneath the leaves:
And years it lies here and dreams in the depth and grieves,
More faithful than mother or father in the light or dark of the leaves.

So, weary of greetings now and the new friend's smile,
Weary in art of the stranger, worn with your wanderer's wile,
Weary of innocence and the husks of Time,
You come, back to the homeland of no-Time,
To ask forgiveness and the patrimony of your crime;

And kneel in the untutored night as to demand
What gift—oh, father, father—from that dissevering hand?)

"And whar's Little Billie?" Joe Drew said.
"Air you crazy," said Big, "and plum outa yore head,
Fer you knows he went West nigh ten long year?"
"Went West," Joe said, "but I seen him here
In the section between the rivers,
Riden up the trace as big as you please
With a long black coat comen down to his knees
And a big black beard comen down to his guts
And silver mountens on his pistol-butts
And he said out West how he done struck
It rich and wuz bringen you back yore luck."
"I shore-God could use some luck," Big Billie said,
But his woman wet her lips and craned her head,

235

And said: "Come riden with a big black beard, you say?"
And Joe: "Oh, it wuz Billie as big as day."
And the old man's eyes bugged out of a sudden and he croaked like a sick bull-frog
         and said: "Come riden with a long black coat?"

The night is still and the grease-lamp low
And the old man's breath comes wheeze and slow.
Oh, the blue flame sucks on the old rag wick
And the old woman's breath comes sharp and quick,
And there isn't a sound under the roof
But her breath's hiss and his breath's puff,
And there isn't a sound outside the door
As they hearken but cannot hear any more
The creak of saddle or the plop of hoof,
For a long time now Joe Drew's been gone
And left them sitting there alone
In the land between the rivers.
And so they sit and breathe and wait
And breathe while the night gets big and late,
And neither of them gives move or stir.
She won't look at him and he won't look at her.
He doesn't look at her but he says: "Git me the spade."

She grabbled with her hands and he dug with the spade
Where leaves let down the dark and shade
In the land between the rivers.
She grabbled like a dog in the hole they made,
But stopped of a sudden and then she said,
"My hand's on his face."
They light up a pine-knot and lean at the place
Where the man in the black coat slumbers and lies
With trash in his beard and dirt on his face;
And the torch-flame shines in his wide-open eyes.

Down the old man leans with the flickering flame
And moves his lips, says: "Tell me his name."

"Ain't Billie, ain't Billie," the old woman cries,
"Oh, it ain't my Billie, fer he wuz little
And helt to my skirt while I stirred the kittle
And called me Mammy and hugged me tight
And come in the house when it fell night."
But the old man leans down with the flickering flame
And croaks: "But tell me his name."

"Oh, he ain't got none, he just come riden
From some fer place whar he'd bin biden.
Ain't got a name and never had none—
But Billie, my Billie, he had one,
And it was Billie, it was his name."
But the old man croaked: "Tell me his name."
"Oh, he ain't got none and it's all the same,
But Billie had one, and he was little
And offen his chin I would wipe the spittle
And wiped the drool and kissed him thar
And counted his toes and kissed him whar
The little black mark was under his tit,
Shaped lak a clover under his left tit,
With a shape fer luck and I'd kiss it—"

The old man blinks in the pine-knot flare
And his mouth comes open like a fish for air,
Then he says right low, "I had nigh fergot."
"Oh, I kissed him on his little luck-spot
And I kissed and he'd laugh as lak as not—"
The old man said: "Git his shirt open."

237

The old woman opened the shirt and there was the birthmark under the left tit.
It was shaped for luck.

(The bee knows, and the eel's cold ganglia burn,
And the sad head lifting to the long return,
Through brumal deeps, in the great unsolsticed coil,
Carries its knowledge, navigator without star,
And under the stars, pure in its clamorous toil,
The goose hoots north where the starlit marshes are.
The salmon heaves at the fall, and, wanderer, you
Heave at the great fall of Time, and gorgeous, gleam
In the powerful arc, and anger and outrage like dew,
In your plunge, fling, and plunge to the thunderous stream:
Back to the silence, back to the pool, back
To the high pool, motionless, and the unmurmuring dream.
And you, wanderer, back,
Brother to pinion and the pious fin that cleave
Their innocence of air and the disinfectant flood
And wing and welter and weave
The long compulsion and the circuit hope
Back,
And bear through that limitless and devouring fluidity
The itch and humble promise which is home.

And the father waits for the son.

The hour is late,
The scene familiar even in shadow,
The transaction brief,
And you, wanderer, back,
After the striving and the wind's word,
To kneel
Here in the evening empty of wind or bird,

238

To kneel in the sacramental silence of evening
At the feet of the old man
Who is evil and ignorant and old,
To kneel
With the little black mark under your heart,
Which is your name,
Which is shaped for luck,
Which is your luck.)

Terror

"*I Volontari Americani Presso Eserciti Stranieri Non Perdono La Cittadinanza.*"
II Messaggero, *Roma, Sabato, 27 Gennaio, 1940.*

Not picnics or pageants or the improbable
Powers of air whose tongues exclaim dominion
And gull the great man to follow his terrible
Star, suffice; not the window-box, or the bird on
The ledge, which means so much to the invalid,
Nor the joy you leaned after, as by the tracks the grass
In the emptiness after the lighted Pullmans fled,
Suffices; nor faces, which, like distraction, pass
Under the street-lamps, teasing to faith or pleasure,
Suffice you, born to no adequate definition of terror.

For yours, like a puppy, is darling and inept,
Though his cold nose brush your hand while you laugh at his clowning;
Or the kitten you sleep with, though once or twice while you slept
It tried to suck your breath, and you dreamed of drowning,
Perjured like Clarence, sluiced from the perilous hatches;
But never of lunar wolf-waste or the arboreal
Malignancy, with the privy breath, which watches
And humps in the dark; but only a dream, after all.
At the worst, you think, with a little twinge of distress,
That contagion may nook in the comforting fur you love to caress.

Though some, unsatisfied and sick, have sought
That immitigable face whose smile is ice,
And fired their hearts like pitch-pine, for they thought
Better flame than the damp worm-tooth of compromise:
So Harry L., my friend, whose whores and gin
Would have dwindled to a slick smile in the drug store

240

But for the absurd contraption of the plane
Which flung on air the unformulable endeavor
While his heart bled speed to lave the applauded name.
The crash was in an old cornfield—not even flame.

So some, whose passionate emptiness and tidal
Lust swayed toward the debris of Madrid,
And left New York to loll in their fierce idyll
Among the olives, where the snipers hid.
And now the North—to seek that visioned face
And polarize their iron of despair,
Who praise no beauty like the boreal grace
Which greens the dead eye under the rocket's flare.
They fight old friends, for their obsession knows
Only the immaculate itch, not human friends or foes.

They sought a secret which fat Franco's Moor,
Hieratic, white-robed, pitiless, might teach,
Who duped and dying but for pride, therefore
Hugged truth which cause or conscience scarcely reach.
As Jacob all night with the angelic foe,
They wrestled him who did not speak, but died,
And wrestle now, by frozen fen and floe,
New Courier, in fury sanctified;
And seek that face which, greasy, frost-breathed, in furs,
Bends to the bomb-sight over bitter Helsingfors.

Blood splashed on the terrorless intellect creates
Corrosive fizzle like the spattered lime,
And its enseamed stew but satiates
Itself, in that lewd and faceless pantomime.
You know, by radio, how hotly the world repeats,
When the brute crowd roars or the blunt boot-heels resound

In the Piazza or the Wilhelmplatz,
The crime of Onan, spilled upon the ground;
You know, whose dear hope Alexis Carrel kept
Alive in a test tube, where it monstrously grew, and slept.

But it is dead, and you now, guiltless, sink
To rest in lobbies, or pace gardens where
The slow god crumbles and the fountains prink,
Nor heed the criminal king, who paints the air
With discoursed madness and protruding eye—
Nor give the alarm, nor ask tonight where sleeps
That head which hooped the jewel Fidelity,
But like an old melon now, in the dank ditch, seeps;
For you crack nuts, while the conscience-stricken stare
Kisses the terror; for you see an empty chair.

Pursuit

The hunchback on the corner, with gum and shoelaces,
Has his own wisdom and pleasures, and may not be lured
To divulge them to you, for he has merely endured
Your appeal for his sympathy and your kind purchases;
And wears infirmity but as the general who turns
Apart, in his famous old greatcoat there on the hill
At dusk when the rapture and cannonade are still,
To muse withdrawn from the dead, from his gorgeous subalterns;
Or stares from the thicket of his familiar pain, like a fawn
That meets you a moment, wheels, in imperious innocence is gone.

Go to the clinic. Wait in the outer room
Where like an old possum the snag-nailed hand will hump
On its knee in murderous patience, and the pomp
Of pain swells like the Indies, or a plum.
And there you will stand, as on the Roman hill,
Stunned by each withdrawn gaze and severe shape,
The first barbarian victor stood to gape
At the sacrificial fathers, white-robed, still;
And even the feverish old Jew stares stern with authority
Till you feel like one who has come too late, or improperly clothed, to a party.

*

The doctor will take you now. He is burly and clean;
Listening, like lover or worshiper, bends at your heart.
He cannot make out just what it tries to impart,
So smiles; says you simply need a change of scene.
Of scene, of solace: therefore Florida,
Where Ponce de Leon clanked among the lilies,
Where white sails skit on blue and cavort like fillies,
And the shoulder gleams white in the moonlit corridor.
A change of love: if love is a groping Godward, though blind,
No matter what crevice, cranny, chink, bright in dark, the pale tentacle find.

In Florida consider the flamingo,
Its color passion but its neck a question.
Consider even that girl the other guests shun
On beach, at bar, in bed, for she may know
The secret you are seeking, after all;
Or the child you humbly sit by, excited and curly,
That screams on the shore at the sea's sunlit hurlyburly,
Till the mother calls its name, toward nightfall.
Till you sit alone: in the dire meridians, off Ireland, in fury
Of spume-tooth and dawnless sea-heave, salt rimes the lookout's devout eye.

Till you sit alone—which is the beginning of error—
Behind you the music and lights of the great hotel:
Solution, perhaps, is public, despair personal,
But history held to your breath clouds like a mirror.
There are many states, and towns in them, and faces,
But meanwhile, the little old lady in black, by the wall,
Admires all the dancers, and tells you how just last fall
Her husband died in Ohio, and damp mists her glasses;
She blinks and croaks, like a toad or a Norn, in the horrible light,
And rattles her crutch, which may put forth a small bloom, perhaps white.

Original Sin: A Short Story

Nodding, its great head rattling like a gourd,
And locks like seaweed strung on the stinking stone,
The nightmare stumbles past, and you have heard
It fumble your door before it whimpers and is gone:
It acts like the old hound that used to snuffle your door and moan.

You thought you had lost it when you left Omaha,
For it seemed connected then with your grandpa, who
Had a wen on his forehead and sat on the veranda
To finger the precious protuberance, as was his habit to do,
Which glinted in sun like rough garnet or the rich old brain bulging through.

But you met it in Harvard Yard as the historic steeple
Was confirming the midnight with its hideous racket,
And you wondered how it had come, for it stood so imbecile,
With empty hands, humble, and surely nothing in pocket:
Riding the rods, perhaps—or Grandpa's will paid the ticket.

You were almost kindly then, in your first homesickness,
As it tortured its stiff face to speak, but scarcely mewed.
Since then you have outlived all your homesickness,
But have met it in many another distempered latitude:
Oh, nothing is lost, ever lost! at last you understood.

It never came in the quantum glare of sun
To shame you before your friends, and had nothing to do
With your public experience or private reformation:
But it thought no bed too narrow—it stood with lips askew
And shook its great head sadly like the abstract Jew.

*

245

Never met you in the lyric arsenical meadows
When children call and your heart goes stone in the bosom—
At the orchard anguish never, nor ovoid horror,
Which is furred like a peach or avid like the delicious plum.
It takes no part in your classic prudence or fondled axiom.

Not there when you exclaimed: "Hope is betrayed by
Disastrous glory of sea-capes, sun-torment of whitecaps
—There must be a new innocence for us to be stayed by."
But there it stood, after all the timetables, all the maps,
In the crepuscular clutter of *always, always,* or *perhaps*.

You have moved often and rarely left an address,
And hear of the deaths of friends with a sly pleasure,
A sense of cleansing and hope which blooms from distress;
But it has not died, it comes, its hand childish, unsure,
Clutching the bribe of chocolate or a toy you used to treasure.

It tries the lock. You hear, but simply drowse:
There is nothing remarkable in that sound at the door.
Later you may hear it wander the dark house
Like a mother who rises at night to seek a childhood picture;
Or it goes to the backyard and stands like an old horse cold in the pasture.

Crime

Envy the mad killer who lies in the ditch and grieves,
Hearing the horns on the highway, and the tires scream.
He tries to remember, and tries, but he cannot seem
To remember what it was he buried under the leaves.

By the steamed lagoon, near the carnivorous orchid,
Pirates hide treasure and mark the place with a skull,
Then lose the map, and roar in pubs with a skinful,
In Devon or Barbados; but remember what they hid.

But what was the treasure he buried? He's too tired to ask it.
An old woman mumbling her gums like incertitude?
The proud stranger who asked the match by the park wood?
Or the child who crossed the park every day with the lunch-basket?

He cannot say, nor formulate the delicious
And smooth convolution of terror, like whipped cream,
Nor the mouth, rounded and white for the lyric scream
Which he never heard, though he still tries, nodding and serious.

His treasure: for years down streets of contempt and trouble,
Hugged under his coat, among sharp elbows and rows
Of eyes hieratic like foetuses in jars.
Or he nursed it unwitting, like a child asleep with a bauble.

Happiness: what the heart wants. That is its fond
Definition, and wants only the peace in God's eye.
Our flame bends in that draft, and that is why
He clutched at the object bright on the bottom of the murky pond.

*

247

All he asked was peace. Past despair and past the uncouth
Violation, he snatched at the fleeting hem, though in error;
Nor gestured before the mind's sycophant mirror,
Nor made the refusal and spat from the secret side of his mouth.

Though a tree for you is a tree, and in the long
Dark, no sibilant tumor inside your enormous
Head, though no walls confer in the silent house,
Nor the eyes of pictures protrude, like snail's, each on its prong,

Yet envy him, for what he buried is buried
By the culvert there, till the boy with the air-gun
In spring, at the violet, comes; nor is ever known
To go on any vacations with him, lend money, break bread.

And envy him, for though the seasons stammer
Past pulse in the yellow throat of the field-lark,
Still memory drips, a pipe in the cellar-dark,
And in its hutch and hole, as when the earth gets warmer,

The cold heart heaves like a toad, and lifts its brow
With that bright jewel you have no use for now;
While puzzled yet, despised with the attic junk, the letter
Names over your name, and mourns under the dry rafter.

Letter from a Coward to a Hero

What did the day bring?
The sharp fragment,
The shard,
The promise half-meant,
The impaired thing,
At dusk the hard word,
Good action by good will marred—
All
In the trampled stall:

    I think you deserved better;
    Therefore I am writing you this letter.

The scenes of childhood were splendid,
And the light that there attended,
But is rescinded:
The cedar,
The lichened rocks,
The thicket where I saw the fox,
And where I swam, the river.
These things are hard
To reconstruct:
The word
Is memory's gelded usufruct.
But piety is simple,
And should be ample.

*

Though late at night we have talked,
I cannot see what ways your feet in childhood walked.
In what purlieus was courage early caulked?

Guns blaze in autumn and
The quail falls and
Empires collide with a bang
That shakes the pictures where they hang
And democracy shows signs of dry rot
And Dives has and Lazarus not
And the time is out of joint,
But a good pointer holds the point
And is not gun-shy.
But I
Am gun-shy.

Though young, I do not like loud noise:
The sudden backfire,
The catcall of boys,
Drums beating for
The big war,
Or clocks that tick at night, and will not stop.
If you should lose your compass and map
Or a mouse get in the wall,
For sleep try love or veronal,
Though some prefer, I know, philology.
Does the airman scream in the flaming trajectory?

You have been strong in love and hate.
Disaster owns less speed than you have got,
But he will cut across the back lot
To lurk and lie in wait.
Admired of children, gathered for their games,
Disaster, like the dandelion, blooms,

And the delicate film is fanned
To seed the shaven lawn.
Rarely, you've been unmanned;
I have not seen your courage put to pawn.

At the blind hour of unaimed grief,
Of addition and subtraction,
Of compromise,
Of the smoky lecher, the thief,
Of regretted action,
At the hour to close the eyes,
At the hour when lights go out in the houses—
Then wind rouses
The kildees from their sodden ground.
Their commentary is part of the wind's sound.
What is that other sound,
Surf or distant cannonade?
You are what you are without our aid.
No doubt, when corridors are dumb
And the bed is made,
It is your custom to recline,
Clutching between the forefinger and thumb
Honor, for death shy valentine.

History

Past crag and scarp,
At length way won:
And done
The chert's sharp
Incision,
The track-flint's bite.
Now done, the belly's lack,
Belt tight
—The shrunk sack,
Corn spent, meats foul,
The dry gut-growl.

Now we have known the last,
And can appraise
Pain past.
We came bad ways,
The watercourses
Dry,
No herb for horses.
(We slew them shamefastly,
Dodging their gaze.)
Sleet came some days,
At night no fuel.

And so, thin-wrapt,
We slept:
Forgot the frosty nostril,
Joints rotten and the ulcered knee,

The cold-kibed heel,
The cracked lip.
It was bad country of no tree,
Of abrupt landslip,
The glacier's snore.
Much man can bear.

How blind the passes were!

And now
We see, below,
The delicate landscape unfurled,
A world
Of ripeness blent, and green,
The fruited earth,
Fire on the good hearth,
The fireside scene.
(Those people have no name,
Who shall know dearth
And flame.)
It is a land of corn and kine,
Of milk
And wine,
And beds that are as silk:
The gentle thigh,
The unlit night-lamp nigh.
This much was prophesied:
We shall possess,
And abide
—Nothing less.
We may not be denied.
The inhabitant shall flee as the fox.
His foot shall be among the rocks.

*

In the new land
Our seed shall prosper, and
In those unsifted times
Our sons shall cultivate
Peculiar crimes,
Having not love, nor hate,
Nor memory.
Though some,
Of all most weary,
Most defective of desire,
Shall grope toward time's cold womb;
In dim pools peer
To see, of some grandsire,
The long and toothèd jawbone greening there.
(O Time, for them the aimless bitch
—Purblind, field-worn,
Slack dugs by the dry thorn torn—
Forever quartering the ground in which
The blank and fanged
Rough certainty lies hid.)

Now at our back
The night wind lifts,
Rain in the wind.
Downward the darkness shifts.
It is the hour for attack.
Wind fondles, far below, the leaves of the land,
Freshening the arbor.
Recall our honor,
And descend.
We seek what end?
The slow dynastic ease,
Travail's cease?

Not pleasure, sure:
Alloy of fact?
The act
Alone is pure.
What appetency knows the flood,
What thirst, the sword?
What name
Sustains the core of flame?
We are the blade,
But not the hand
By which the blade is swayed.
Time falls, but has no end.
Descend!

The gentle path suggests our feet;
The bride's surrender will be sweet.
We shall essay
The rugged ritual, but not of anger.
Let us go down before
Our thews are latched in the myth's languor,
Our hearts with fable gray.

End of Season

Leave now the beach, and even that perfect friendship
—Hair frosting, careful teeth—that came, oh! late,
Late, late, almost too late: that thought like a landslip;
Or only the swimmer's shape for which you would wait,
Bemused and pure among the bright umbrellas, while
Blue mountains breathed and the dark boys cried their bird-throated syllable.

Leave beach, *spiagga, playa, plage,* or *spa,*
Where beginnings are always easy; or leave, even,
The Springs where your grandpa went in Arkansas
To purge the rheumatic guilt of beef and bourbon,
And slept like a child, nor called out with the accustomed nightmare,
But lolled his old hams, stained hands, in that Lethe, as others, others, before.

For waters wash our guilt and dance in the sun—
And the prophet, hairy and grim in the leonine landscape,
Came down to Jordan; toward moon-set de Leon
Woke while, squat, Time clucked like the darkling ape;
And Dante's *duca,* smiling in the blessèd clime,
With rushes, sea-wet, wiped from that sad brow the infernal grime.

You'll come, you'll come! and with the tongue gone wintry
You'll greet in town the essential face, which now wears
The mask of travel, smudge of history.
Then wordless, each one clasps, and stammering, stares:
You will have to learn a new language to say what is to say,
But it will never be useful in schoolroom, customs, or café.

✳

256

For purity was wordless, and perfection
But the bridegroom's sleep or the athlete's marble dream,
And the annual sacrament of sea and sun,
Which browns the face and heals the heart, will seem
Silence, expectant to the answer, which is Time:
For all our conversation is index to our common crime.

On the last day swim far out, should the doctor permit
—Crawl, trudgeon, breast—or deep and wide-eyed, dive
Down the glaucous glimmer where no voice can visit.
But the mail lurks in the box at the house where you live:
Summer's wishes, winter's wisdom—you must think
On the true nature of Hope, whose eye is round and does not wink.

Ransom

Old houses, and new-fangled violence;
Old bottles but new wine, and newly spilled.
Doom has, we know, no shape but the shape of air.
That much for us the red-armed augurs spelled,
Or flights of fowl lost early in the long air.

The mentioned act: barbarous, bloody, extreme,
And fraught with bane. The actors: nameless and
With faces turned (I cannot make them out).
Christ bled, indeed, but after fasting and
Bad diet of the poor; wherefore thin blood came out.

What wars and lecheries! and the old zeal
Yet unfulfilled, unrarefied, unlaced.
At night the old man coughs: thus history
Strikes sum, ere dawn in rosy buskins laced
Delivers cool with dew the recent news-story.

Defeat is possible, and the stars rise.
Our courage needs, perhaps, new definition.
By night, my love, and noon, infirm of will
And young, we may endeavor definition;
Though frail as the claspèd dream beneath the blanket's wool.

To a Friend Parting

Endure friend-parting yet, old soldier,
Scarred the heart, and wry: the wild plum,
Rock-rent, ax-bit, has known with the year bloom,
And tides, the neap and spring, bear faithfully.
Much you have done in honor, though wrathfully.
That, we supposed, was your doom.

O you who by the grove and shore walked
With us, your heart unbraced yet unbetrayed,
Recall: the said, the unsaid, though chaff the said
And backward blown. We saw above the lake
The hawk tower, his wings the light take.
What answer to our dread?

Follow the defiles down. Forget not,
When journey-bated the nag, rusty the steel,
The horny clasp of hands your hands now seal;
And prayers of friends, ere this, kept powder dry.
Rough country of no birds, the tracks sly:
Thus faith has lived, we feel.

Eidolon

All night, in May, dogs barked in the hollow woods;
Hoarse, from secret huddles of no light,
By moonlit bole, hoarse, the dogs gave tongue.
In May, by moon, no moon, thus: I remember
Of their far clamor the throaty, infatuate timbre.

The boy, all night, lay in the black room,
Tick-straw, all night, harsh to the bare side.
Staring, he heard; the clotted dark swam slow.
Far off, by wind, no wind, unappeasable riot
Provoked, resurgent, the bosom's nocturnal disquiet.

What hungers kept the house? under the rooftree
The boy; the man, clod-heavy, hard hand uncurled;
The old man, eyes wide, spittle on his beard.
In dark was crushed the may-apple: plunging, the rangers
Of dark remotelier belled their unhouseled angers.

Dogs quartered the black woods: blood black on
May-apple at dawn, old beech-husk. And trails are lost
By rock, in ferns lost, by pools unlit.
I heard the hunt. Who saw, in darkness, how fled
The white eidolon from the fanged commotion rude?

Revelation

Because he had spoken harshly to his mother,
The day became astonishingly bright,
The enormity of distance crept to him like a dog now,
And earth's own luminescence seemed to repel the night.

Rent was the roof like loud paper to admit
Sun-sulphurous splendor where had been before
But a submarine glimmer by kindly countenances lit,
As slow, phosphorescent dignities light the ocean floor.

By walls, by walks, chrysanthemum and aster,
All hairy, fat-petaled species, lean, confer,
And his ears, and heart, should burn at that insidious whisper
Which concerns him so, he knows; but he cannot make out the words.

The peacock screamed, and his feathered fury made
Legend shake, all day, while the sky ran pale as milk;
That night, all night, the buck rabbit stamped in the moonlit glade,
And the owl's brain glowed like a coal in the grove's combustible dark.

When Sulla smote and Rome was racked, Augustine
Recalled how Nature, shuddering, tore her gown,
And kind changed kind, and the blunt herbivorous tooth dripped blood;
At Duncan's death, at Dunsinane, chimneys blew down.

*

261

But, oh! his mother was kinder than ever Rome,
Dearer than Duncan—no wonder, then, Nature's frame
Thrilled in voluptuous hemispheres far off from his home;
But not in terror: only as the bride, as the bride.

In separateness only does love learn definition,
Though Brahma smiles beneath the dappled shade,
Though tears, that night, wet the pillow where the boy's head was laid,
Dreamless of splendid antipodal agitation;

And though across what tide and tooth Time is,
He was to lean back toward that irredeemable face,
He would think, than Sulla more fortunate, how once he had learned
Something important above love, and about love's grace.

MEXICO IS A FOREIGN COUNTRY:
FOUR STUDIES IN NATURALISM

I Butterflies over the Map

Butterflies, over the map of Mexico,
Over jungle and somnolent, sonorous mountains, flitter,
Over the death-gaudy dog whose spangles the sun makes glitter,
And over the red lines which are the highways where you will go.

The highways are scenic, like destiny marked in red,
And the faithful heart inside you purrs like a cat;
While distance drowses and blinks and broods its enormous fiat,
Butterflies dream gyres round the precious flower which is your head.

Their colors are astonishing, and so
Like Brutus, you wrathless rose and, robed in the pure
Idea, smote, and fled, while benches burned, from the clamor:
The black limousine was not detected at Laredo.

Tragedy is a dance, as Brutus knew;
But when a little child dies in Jalisco,
They lay the corpse, pink cloth on its face, in the patio,
And bank it with blossoms, yellow, red, and the Virgin's blue.

The pink cloth is useful to foil the flies, which are not few.

I I   The World Comes Galloping: A True Story

By the ruined arch, where the bougainvillea bled,
And pigeons simmered and shat in the barbaric vine
And made a noise like Plato in the barbaric vine,
He stood: old.
Old, bare feet on stone, and the serape's rose
Unfolded in the garden of his rags;
Old, and all his history hung from his severe face
As from his frame the dignity of rags.

We could not see his history, we saw
Him.
And he saw us, but could not see we stood
Huddled in our history and stuck out hand for alms.

But he could give us nothing, and asked for nothing,
Whose figure, sharp against the blue lake and violet mountains,
Was under the arch, the vine, the violet blue vulgarity of sky.
He ate a peach and wiped the pulp across his gums;
His mouth was no less ruinous than the arch.

*

Then at the foot of that long street,
Between the pastel stucco and the feathery pepper trees,
Horse and horseman, sudden as light, and loud,
Appeared,
And up the rise, banging the cobbles like castanets,
Lashed in their fury and fever,
Plunged:
Wall-eyed and wheezing, the lurching hammer-head,
The swaying youth, and flapping from bare heels,
The great wheel-spurs of the Conquistador.
Plunged past us, and were gone:
The crow-bait mount, the fly-bit man.

So the old one, dropping his peach-pit, spat;
Regarding the street's astonishing vacancy, said:
"Viene galopando"—and spat again—"el mundo."

III   Small Soldiers with Drum in Large Landscape

The little soldiers thread the hills.
Remote, the white Sierra nods
Like somnolent ice cream piled up
To tempt a tourist's taste, or God's.

I saw them in the Plaza when
They huddled there like hens, at dawn,
And forming ranks, took time to gouge
Sleep from their eyes, and spit, and yawn.

Their bearing lacked ferocity.
Their eyes were soft, their feet were splayed,
And dirt, no doubt, behind the ears
Did them no credit on parade.

They did not tell me why they march—
To give some cattle-thief a scare
Or make their captain happy or
Simply take the mountain air.

But now two hours off, they move
Across the scene, and to the eye
Give interest, and focus for
The composition's majesty.

✻

The little drum goes rum-tum-tum,
The little hearts go rat-tat-tat,
And I am I, and they are they,
And *this* is *this,* and *that* is *that,*

And the single pine is black upon
The crag; and the buzzard, absolute
In the sun's great gold eye, hangs;
And leaf is leaf, and root is root;

And the wind has neither home nor hope;
And cause is cause, effect, effect;
And all Nature's jocund atoms bounce
In tune to keep the world intact.

And shrouded in the coats and buttons,
The atoms bounce, and under the sky,
Under the mountain's gaze, maintain
The gallant little formulae

Which sweat and march, and marching, go
On errands which I have not guessed,
Though here I stand and watch them go
From dawn to dark, from East to West,

From *what* to *what,* from *if* to *when,*
From ridge to ridge, and cross the wide
Landscape of probability.
They cross the last ridge now, and hide
※

In valleys where the unprinted dust
Yearns for the foot it does not know;
They march under the same sun,
Appear once more, are gone, but go

Across the high waste of the mind,
Across the distance in the breast,
And climbing hazier heights, proceed
To a bivouac in a farther West.

I V   The Mango on the Mango Tree

The mango on the mango tree—
I look at it, it looks at me,
And thus we share our guilt in decent secrecy

(As once in the crowd I met a face
Whose lineaments were my disgrace
And whose own shame my forehead bore from place to place).

The mango is a great gold eye,
Like God's, set in the leafy sky
To harry heart, block blood, freeze feet, if I would fly.

For God has set it there to spy
And make report, and here am I,
A cosmic Hawkshaw to track down its villainy.

Gumshoe, *agent provocateur,*
Stool, informer, whisperer
—Each pours his tale into the Great Schismatic's ear.

For God well works the Roman plan,
Divide and rule, mango and man,
And on hate's axis the great globe grinds in its span.

I do not know the mango's crime
In its far place and different time,
Nor does it know mine committed in a frostier clime.

✲

But what to God's were ours, who pay,
Drop by slow drop, day after day,
Until His monstrous, primal guilt be washed away,

Who till that time must thus atone
In pulp and pit, in flesh and bone,
By our vicarious sacrifice fault not our own?

For, ah, I do not know what word
The mango might hear, or if I've heard
A breath like *pardon, pardon,* when its stiff lips stirred.

If there were a word that it could give,
Or if I could only say *forgive,*
Then we might lift the Babel curse by which we live,

And I could leap and laugh and sing
And it could leap, and everything
Take hands with us and pace the music in a ring,

And sway like the multitudinous wheat
In a blessedness so long in forfeit—
Blest in that blasphemy of love we cannot now repeat.

Monologue at Midnight

Among the pines we ran and called
In joy and innocence, and still
Our voices doubled in the high
Green groining our simplicity.

And we have heard the windward hound
Bell in the frosty vault of dark.
(Then what pursuit?) How soundlessly
The maple shed its pollen in the sun.

Season by season from the skein
Unwound, of earth and of our pleasure;
And always at the side, like guilt,
Our shadows over the grasses moved,

Or moved across the moonlit snow;
And move across the grass or snow.
Or was it guilt? Philosophers
Loll in their disputatious ease.

The match flame sudden in the gloom
Is lensed within each watching eye
Less intricate, less small, than in
One heart the other's image is.

*

The hound, the echo, flame, or shadow—
And which am I and which are you?
And are we Time who flee so fast,
Or stone who stand, and thus endure?

Our mathematic yet has use
For the integers of blessedness:
Listen! the poor deluded cock
Salutes the coldness of no dawn.

Bearded Oaks

The oaks, how subtle and marine,
Bearded, and all the layered light
Above them swims; and thus the scene,
Recessed, awaits the positive night.

So, waiting, we in the grass now lie
Beneath the languorous tread of light:
The grasses, kelp-like, satisfy
The nameless motions of the air.

Upon the floor of light, and time,
Unmurmuring, of polyp made,
We rest; we are, as light withdraws,
Twin atolls on a shelf of shade.

Ages to our construction went,
Dim architecture, hour by hour:
And violence, forgot now, lent
The present stillness all its power.

The storm of noon above us rolled,
Of light the fury, furious gold,
The long drag troubling us, the depth:
Dark is unrocking, unrippling, still.
＊

Passion and slaughter, ruth, decay
Descend, minutely whispering down,
Silted down swaying streams, to lay
Foundation for our voicelessness.

All our debate is voiceless here,
As all our rage, the rage of stone;
If hope is hopeless, then fearless is fear,
And history is thus undone.

Our feet once wrought the hollow street
With echo when the lamps were dead
At windows, once our headlight glare
Disturbed the doe that, leaping, fled.

I do not love you less that now
The caged heart makes iron stroke,
Or less that all that light once gave
The graduate dark should now revoke.

We live in time so little time
And we learn all so painfully,
That we may spare this hour's term
To practice for eternity.

Picnic Remembered

That day, so innocent appeared
The leaf, the hill, the sky, to us,
Their structures so harmonious
And pure, that all we had endured
Seemed the quaint disaster of a child,
Now cupboarded, and all the wild
Grief canceled; so with what we feared.

We stood among the painted trees:
The amber light laved them, and us;
Or light then so untremulous,
So steady, that our substances,
Twin flies, were as in amber tamed
With our perfections stilled and framed
To mock Time's marveling after-spies.

Joy, strongest medium, then buoyed
Us when we moved, as swimmers, who,
Relaxed, resign them to the flow
And pause of their unstained flood.
Thus wrapped, sustained, we did not know
How darkness darker staired below;
Or knowing, but half understood.

*

The bright deception of that day!
When we so readily could gloze
All pages opened to expose
The truth we never would betray;
But darkness on the landscape grew
As in our bosoms darkness, too;
And that was what we took away.

And it abides, and may abide:
Though ebbed from the region happier mapped,
Our hearts, like hollow stones, have trapped
A corner of that brackish tide.
The jaguar breath, the secret wrong,
The curse that curls the sudden tongue,
We know; for fears have fructified.

Or are we dead, that we, unmanned,
Are vacant, and our clearest souls
Are sped where each with each patrols,
In still society, hand in hand,
That scene where we, too, wandered once
Who now inherit a new province,
Love's limbo, this lost under-land?

The *then,* the *now:* each cenotaph
Of the other, and proclaims it dead.
Or is the soul a hawk that, fled
On glimmering wings past vision's path,
Reflects the last gleam to us here
Though sun is sunk and darkness near
—Uncharted Truth's high heliograph?

Love's Parable

As kingdoms after civil broil,
Long faction-bit and sore unmanned,
Unlaced, unthewed by lawless toil,
Will welcome to the cheering strand
A prince whose tongue, not understood,
Yet frames a new felicity,
And alien, seals domestic good:
Once, each to each, such aliens, we.

That time, each was the other's sun,
Ecliptic's charter, system's core;
Locked in its span, the wandering one,
Though colder grown, might yet endure
Ages unnumbered, for it fed
On light and heat flung from the source
Of light that lit dark as it fled:
Wonder of dull astronomers.

No wonder then to us it was!
For miracle was daily food—
That darkness fled through darklessness
And endless light the dark pursued:
No wonder then, for we had found
Love's mystery, then still unspent,
That substance long in grossness bound
Might bud into love's accident.

✻

277

Then miracle was corner-cheap;
And we, like ignorant quarriers,
Ransacked the careless earth to heap
For highways our most precious ores;
Or like the blockhead masons who
Burnt Rome's best grandeur for its lime,
And for their slattern hovels threw
Down monuments of a nobler time.

We did not know what worth we owned,
Or know what ambient atmosphere
We breathed, who daily then postponed
A knowledge that, now bought too dear,
Is but ironic residue:
As gouty pang and tarnished vest
Remind the wastrel bankrupt who,
For gut and back, let substance waste.

That all the world proportionate
And joyful seemed, did but consent
That all unto our garden state
Of innocence was innocent;
And all on easy axle roved
That now, ungeared, perturbed turns,
For joy sought joy then when we loved,
As iron to the magnet yearns.

✳

But we have seen the fungus eyes
Of misery spore in the night,
And marked, of friends, the malices
That stain, like smoke, the day's fond light,
And marked how ripe injustice flows,
How ulcerous, how acid, then
How proud flesh on the sounder grows
Till rot engross the estate of men;

And marked, within, the inward sore
Of self that cankers at the bone,
Contempt of the very love we bore
And hatred of the good once known
—So weakness has become our strength,
And strength, confused, can but reject
Its object, so that we at length,
Itching and slumwise, each other infect.

Are we but mirror to the world?
Or does the world our ruin reflect,
Or is our gazing beauty spoiled
But by the glass' flawed defect?
What fault? What cause? What matter for
The hurled leaf where the wind was brewed,
Or matter for the pest-bit whore
What coin her virtue first beshrewed?

*

O falling-off! O peace composed
Within my kingdom when your reign
Was fulgent-full! and nought opposed
Your power, that slack is, but again
May sway my sullen elements,
And bend ambition to his place.
That hope: for there are testaments
That men, by prayer, have mastered grace.

Late Subterfuge

The year dulls toward its eaves-dripping end.
We have kept honor yet, or lost a friend;
Observed at length the inherited defect;
Known error's pang—but then, what man is perfect?
The grackles, yellow-beaked, beak-southward, fly
To the ruined ricelands south, leaving empty our sky.

This year was time for decision to be made.
No time to waste, we said, and so we said:
This year is time. Our grief can be endured,
For we, at least, are men, being inured
To wrath, to the unjust act, if need, to blood;
And we have faith that from evil blooms good.

Our feet in the sopping woods will make no sound,
The winter's rot begun, the fox in ground,
The snake cold-coiled, secret in cane the weasel.
In pairs we walk, heads bowed to the long drizzle—
With women some, and take their rain-cold kiss;
We say to ourselves we learn some strength from this.

Man Coming of Age

What rime, what tinsel pure and chill,
At dawn defines the new-spied hill?

This brilliance in the night was wrought:
Of dark and cold a dead world caught
Such light that glitters out of thought.

So settles on a dying face,
After the retch and spasm, grace.

(A grace like that did not belong
In the room of no-love, fret, and wrong:
The watchers sat heavy, night was long.)

Now standing on his own doorsill,
He views the woods that crest the hill,

And asks: "Was it I who roamed to prove
My heart beneath the unwhispering grove
In a season greener and of more love?"

And was it he? Now let him stride
With cramped knee the slant hillside,

Pondering what ways he used to know,
Seeking under the snowy bough
That frail reproachful *alter ego*.

*

Walker in woods that bear no leaf,
Climber of rocks, assume your grief

And go! lest he, before you tread
That ground once sweetly tenanted,
Like mist, down the glassy gloom be fled.

The Garden

On prospect of a fine day in early autumn

How kind, how secret, now the sun
Will bless this garden frost has won,
And touch once more, as once it used,
The furled boughs by cold bemused.
Though summered brilliance had but room
In blossom, now the leaves will bloom
Their time, and take from milder sun
An unreviving benison.

  No marbles whitely gaze among
These paths where gilt the late pear hung:
But branches interlace to frame
The avenue of stately flame
Where yonder, far more bold and pure
Than marble, gleams the sycamore,
Of argent torse and cunning shaft
Propped nobler than the sculptor's craft.

  The hand that crooked upon the spade
Here plucked the peach, and thirst allayed;
Here lovers paused before the kiss,
Instructed of what ripeness is:
Where all who came might stand to prove
The grace of this imperial grove,
Now jay and cardinal debate,
Like twin usurpers, the ruined state.

✳

But he who sought, not love, but peace
In such rank plot could take no ease:
Now poised between the two alarms
Of summer's lusts and winter's harms,
Only for him these precincts wait
In sacrament that can translate
All things that fed luxurious sense
From appetite to innocence.

The Return: An Elegy

The east wind finds the gap bringing rain:
Rain in the pine wind shaking the stiff pine.
Beneath the wind the hollow gorges whine
The pines decline
Slow film of rain creeps down the loam again
Where the blind and nameless bones recline.

    they are conceded to the earth's absolute chemistry
    they burn like faggots in—of damp and dark—the monstrous bulging flame.
    calcium phosphate lust speculation faith treachery
    it walked upright with habitation and a name
    tell me its name

The pines, black, like combers plunge with spray
Lick the wind's unceasing keel
It is not long till day
The boughs like hairy swine in slaughter squeal.
They lurch beneath the thunder's livid heel.
The pines, black, snore *what does the wind say?*

    tell me its name

I have a name: I am not blind.
Eyes, not blind, press to the Pullman pane
Survey the driving dark and silver taunt of rain.
What will I find
What will I find beyond the snoring pine?
O eyes locked blind in death's immaculate design
Shall fix their last distrust in mine

*

give me the nickels off your eyes
from your hands the violets
let me bless your obsequies
if you possessed conveniently enough three eyes
then I could buy a pack of cigarettes

In gorges where the dead fox lies the fern
Will rankest loop the battened frond and fall
Above the bare tushed jaws that turn
Their insolence unto the gracious catafalque and pall.
It will be the season when milkweed blossoms burn.

the old bitch is dead
what have I said!
I have only said what the wind said
wind shakes a bell the hollow head

By dawn, the wind, the blown rain
Will cease their antique concitation.
It is the hour when old ladies cough and wake,
The chair, the table, take their form again
And earth begins the matinal exhalation

does my mother wake

Pines drip without motion
The hairy boughs no longer shake
Shaggy mist, crookbacked, ascends
Round hairy boughs the mist with shaggy fingers bends.
No wind: no rain:
Why do the steady pines complain?
Complain
*

the old fox is dead
what have I said

Locked in the roaring cubicle
Over the mountains through darkness hurled
I race the daylight's westward cycle
Across the groaning rooftree of the world.
The mist is furled.

   a hundred years they took this road
   the lank hunters then men hard-eyed with hope:
   ox breath whitened the chill air: the goad
   fell: here on the western slope
   the hungry people the lost ones took their abode
   here they took their stand:
   alders bloomed on the road to the new land
   here is the house the broken door the shed
   the old fox is dead

The wheels hum hum
The wheels: I come I come
Whirl out of space through time O wheels
Pursue down backward time the ghostly parallels
Pursue past culvert cut embankment semaphore
Pursue down gleaming hours that are no more.
The pines, black, snore

   turn backward turn backward O time in your flight
   and make me a child again just for tonight
   good lord he's wet the bed come bring a light

✳

What grief has the mind distilled?
The heart is unfulfilled
The hoarse pine stilled
I cannot pluck
Out of this land of pine and rock
Of red bud their season not yet gone
If I could pluck
(In drouth the lizard will blink on the hot limestone)

    the old fox is dead
    what is said is said
    heaven rest the hoary head
    what have I said!
    . . . I have only said what the wind said
    honor thy father and mother in the days of thy youth
    for time uncoils like the cottonmouth

If I could pluck
Out of the dark that whirled
Over the hoarse pine over the rock
Out of the mist that furled
Could I stretch forth like God the hand and gather
For you my mother
If I could pluck
Against the dry essential of tomorrow
To lay upon the breast that gave me suck
Out of the dark the dark and swollen orchid of this sorrow.

KENTUCKY MOUNTAIN FARM

I Rebuke of the Rocks

Now on you is the hungry equinox,
O little stubborn people of the hill,
The season of the obscene moon whose pull
Disturbs the sod, the rabbit, the lank fox,
Moving the waters, the boar's dull blood,
And the acrid sap of the ironwood.

But breed no tender thing among the rocks.
Rocks are too old under the mad moon,
Renouncing passion by the strength that locks
The eternal agony of fire in stone.

Then quit yourselves as stone and cease
To break the weary stubble-field for seed;
Let not the naked cattle bear increase,
Let barley wither and the bright milkweed.
Instruct the heart, lean men, of a rocky place
That even the little flesh and fevered bone
May keep the sweet sterility of stone.

I I At the Hour of the Breaking of the Rocks

Beyond the wrack and eucharist of snow
The tortured and reluctant rock again
Receives the sunlight and the tarnished rain.
Such is the hour of sundering we know,
Who on the hills have seen stand and pass
Stubbornly the taciturn
Lean men that of all things alone
Were, not as water or the febrile grass,
Figured in kinship to the savage stone.

The hills are weary, the lean men have passed;
The rocks are stricken, and the frost has torn
Away their ridged fundaments at last,
So that the fractured atoms now are borne
Down shifting waters to the tall, profound
Shadow of the absolute deeps,
Wherein the spirit moves and never sleeps
That held the foot among the rocks, that bound
The tired hand upon the stubborn plow,
Knotted the flesh unto the hungry bone,
The redbud to the charred and broken bough,
And strung the bitter tendons of the stone.

I I I   History Among the Rocks

There are many ways to die
Here among the rocks in any weather:
Wind, down the eastern gap, will lie
Level along the snow, beating the cedar,
And lull the drowsy head that it blows over
To startle a cold and crystalline dream forever.

The hound's black paw will print the grass in May,
And sycamores rise down a dark ravine,
Where a creek in flood, sucking the rock and clay,
Will tumble the laurel, the sycamore away.
Think how a body, naked and lean
And white as the splintered sycamore, would go
Tumbling and turning, hushed in the end,
With hair afloat in waters that gently bend
To ocean where the blind tides flow.

Under the shadow of ripe wheat,
By flat limestone, will coil the copperhead,
Fanged as the sunlight, hearing the reaper's feet.
But there are other ways, the lean men said:
In these autumn orchards once young men lay dead—
Gray coats, blue coats. Young men on the mountainside
Clambered, fought. Heels muddied the rocky spring.
Their reason is hard to guess, remembering
Blood on their black mustaches in moonlight.
Their reason is hard to guess and a long time past:
The apple falls, falling in the quiet night.

I V   The Return

Burly and clean, with bark in umber scrolled
About the sunlit bole's own living white,
The sycamore stood, drenched in the autumn light.
The same old tree. Again the timeless gold
Broad leaf released the tendoned bough, and slow,
Uncertain as a casual memory,
Wavered aslant the ripe unmoving air.
Up from the whiter bough, the bluer sky,
That glimmered in the water's depth below,
A richer leaf rose to the other there.
They touched; with the gentle clarity of dream,
Bosom to bosom, burned on the quiet stream.

But, backward heart, you have no voice to call
Your image back, the vagrant image again.
The tree, the leaf falling, the stream, and all
Familiar faithless things would yet remain
Voiceless. And he, who had loved as well as most,
Might have foretold it thus, for well he knew
How, glimmering, a buried world is lost
In the water's riffle or the wind's flaw;
How his own image, perfect and deep
And small within loved eyes, had been forgot,
Her face being turned, or when those eyes were shut
Past light in that fond accident of sleep.

Pondy Woods

The buzzards over Pondy Woods
Achieve the blue tense altitudes,
Black figments that the woods release,
Obscenity in form and grace,
Drifting high through the pure sunshine
Till the sun in gold decline.

Big Jim Todd was a slick black buck
Laying low in the mud and muck
Of Pondy Woods when the sun went down
In gold, and the buzzards tilted down
A windless vortex to the black-gum trees
To sit along the quiet boughs,
Devout and swollen, at their ease.

By the buzzard roost Big Jim Todd
Listened for hoofs on the corduroy road
Or for the foul and sucking sound
A man's foot makes on the marshy ground.
Past midnight, when the moccasin
Slipped from the log and, trailing in
Its obscured waters, broke
The dark algae, one lean bird spoke.

*

"Nigger, you went this afternoon
For your Saturday spree at the Blue Goose saloon,
So you've got on your Sunday clothes,
On your big splay feet got patent-leather shoes.
But a buzzard can smell the thing you've done;
The posse will get you—run, nigger, run—
There's a fellow behind you with a big shot-gun.
Nigger, nigger, you'll sweat cold sweat
In your patent-leather shoes and Sunday clothes
When down your track the steeljacket goes
Mean and whimpering over the wheat.

"Nigger, your breed ain't metaphysical."
The buzzard coughed. His words fell
In the darkness, mystic and ambrosial.
"But we maintain our ancient rite,
Eat the gods by day and prophesy by night.
We swing against the sky and wait;
You seize the hour, more passionate
Than strong, and strive with time to die—
With Time, the beaked tribe's astute ally.

"The Jew-boy died. The Syrian vulture swung
Remotely above the cross whereon he hung
From dinner-time to supper-time, and all
The people gathered there watched him until
The lean brown chest no longer stirred,
Then idly watched the slow majestic bird
That in the last sun above the twilit hill
Gleamed for a moment at the height and slid
Down the hot wind and in the darkness hid.
Nigger, regard the circumstance of breath:
Non omnis moriar, the poet saith."

✻

Pedantic, the bird clacked its gray beak,
With a Tennessee accent to the classic phrase;
Jim understood, and was about to speak,
But the buzzard drooped one wing and filmed the eyes.

At dawn unto the Sabbath wheat he came,
That gave to the dew its faithless yellow flame
From kindly loam in recollection of
The fires that in the brutal rock once strove.
To the ripe wheat fields he came at dawn.
Northward the printed smoke stood quiet above
The distant cabins of Squiggtown.
A train's far whistle blew and drifted away
Coldly; lucid and thin the morning lay
Along the farms, and here no sound
Touched the sweet earth miraculously stilled.
Then down the damp and sudden wood there belled
The musical white-throated hound.

In Pondy Woods in the August drouth
Lurk fever and the cottonmouth.
And buzzards over Pondy Woods
Achieve the blue tense altitudes,
Drifting high in the pure sunshine
Till the sun in gold decline;
Then golden and hieratic through
The night their eyes burn two by two.

Letter of a Mother

Under the green lamplight her letter there
Lies among cluttered papers, rusted pens,
Books and handkerchiefs, tobacco tins.
Shuffle of feet ascends the darkened stair.

The son, defined upon the superscription,
Inherits now his cubicled domain,
And reads. Indeed, should he regret again
The loneliness in time's slow mitigation?

Or spell the name, which is himself, and say:
"By now this woman's milk is out of me.
I have a debt of flesh, assuredly,
Which score the mintage of the breath might pay—

"A certain weight of cunning flesh devised
So hunger is bred in the bitter bone
To cleave about this precious skeleton
Held mortmain of her womb and merchandised

"Unto the dark: a subtile engine, propped
In the sutured head beneath the coronal seam,
Whose illegal prodigality of dream
In shaking the escheat heart is quick estopped.

✳

"Such is the substance of this legacy:
A fragile vision fed of acrid blood,
Whose sweet process may bloom in gratitude
For the worthier gift of her mortality."

But still the flesh cries out unto the black
Void, across the plains insistently
Where rivers wash their wastage to the sea—
The mother flesh that cannot summon back

The tired child it would again possess
As shall a womb more tender than her own
That builds not tissue or the little bone,
But dissolves them to itself in weariness.

To a Face in a Crowd

Brother, my brother, whither do you pass?
Unto what hill at dawn, unto what glen,
Where among the rocks the faint lascivious grass
Fingers in lust the arrogant bones of men?

Beside what bitter waters will you go
Where the lean gulls of your heart along the shore
Rehearse to the cliffs the rhetoric of their woe?
In dream, perhaps, I have seen your face before.

A certain night has borne both you and me;
We are the children of an ancient band
Broken between the mountains and the sea.
A cromlech marks for you that utmost strand

And you must find the dolorous place they stood.
Of old I know that shore, that dim terrain,
And know how black and turbulent the blood
Will beat through iron chambers of the brain

When at your back the taciturn tall stone,
Which is your fathers' monument and mark,
Repeats the waves' implacable monotone,
Ascends the night and propagates the dark.

*

Men there have lived who wrestled with the ocean;
I was afraid—the polyp was their shroud.
I was afraid. That shore of your decision
Awaits beyond this street where in the crowd

Your face is blown, an apparition, past.
Renounce the night as I, and we must meet
As weary nomads in this desert at last,
Borne in the lost procession of these feet.

DATE DUE

NOV 14 '75			
JUL 21 '77			
MAR 22 '78			
NOV 01 1993			
OCT 27 1993			
GAYLORD			PRINTED IN U.S.A.